From Anger
To Contentment

Six Skills For
Peaceful Living

Frank Bohannan

Program Director
Anger Solutions Network

Anger Solutions Networks, Inc.

900 NE Loop 410, Suite D-307
San Antonio, TX 78209
210-804-0085
Fax 210-804-0086

Go to our website for additional products, services, and information.
www.lifeskillsforliving.org

Cover Design by Troy LeBlanc
Graphics: Elyon Media
Published by Elyon Media
www.elyonmedia.com

ISBN-13:
978-0692718339 (Elyon Media Group LLC)

ISBN-10:
0692718338

Printed in the United States of America

From Anger To Contentment

Praise for From Anger To Contentment

We live in an angry world, comprised of angry people. So often a person may not even be aware of how their anger is affecting their mental health and destroying their relationships. *From Anger To Contentment* provides a practical guide in identifying personal problem areas in the expression of anger and demonstrates sensible techniques for change. *Patricia D. Mirrer LCSW*

Lost with no direction is how we often live. I know this because I lived this way for 42 years. We get mad, hurt, angry, and disappointed with life. Thankfully, there is a better way of dealing with life issues. The book you are holding is like a map for your life. Although it will not stop problems from coming, it will teach you how to handle situations in a healthier way. The tools will help you turn anger to peacefulness. Change is possible, but one has to be willing to put what they have learned into action. Once you put into action what you learn the most amazing thing will start to happen. It will not only improve your life, but others around you will be impacted positively. Don't wait to change because tomorrow is not promised. *Gloria Ofelia Davila, Facilitator for Life Skills for the Living*

This book has been painstakingly developed over many years in real-world scenarios with the input of dozens of volunteers, professionals, and administrators. Having been tested and utilized by some of society's most ravaged and powerless--prisoners, substance abusers, mentally ill, and homeless--this material will have a meaningful impact with significant outcomes for virtually anyone. *Gene Hildabrand, Communications Director, Sweep Over SA!*

Today's need for this book could not be more timely in all it stands for and can provide to any person seeking to develop practical life skills and change the destructive results of negative anger in their / our daily lives. Lives will and are being impacted for positive change with understanding and the desire that there is a better way. This is a practical guide, a road map, to effect change in our lives as applied one day at a time, remembering to never give up in the process, again, one day at a time. I am thankful to see this publication now available and am prayerfully seeking God's blessing on each person who receives it and His miraculous provision in lives being changed through it.
Terry S. Warth, SIOR, Vice President, Brokerage Services for Industrial Properties

Having taught the proven principles of this book for over six years in a tough jail environment, I know they work. They have universal application for all of us. Once we realize that we are all genetically programmed with this powerful, basic survival emotion called anger, we can learn to apply the practical, common sense tools presented here. The key is understanding the basic mechanism, how to identify the negative emotions that "trigger" destructive anger, and apply the tools presented here. This book helps you build a starter tool box to which you can add tools unique to you. Get started! *William F. Daugherty, COL (Ret), U.S. Army, President, WFD Enterprises, Inc.*

I am the oldest and one of five siblings. We grew up in with a very angry and abusive father. Our mother took the brunt of the abuse. It almost destroyed our entire family. When I was introduced to Life Skills for Living and their 'Anger Management Program' I knew this program had to be shared with families that are suffering from anger and abuse. This program can greatly help in changing the lives of people that are angry and full of rage. I so wish this program was around for my father. I highly endorse this book. Read, study it and put it into practice. It can make a profound difference. *Eric Eisbrenner, Businessman, Entrepreneur*

The goals and concepts in this book are easily identifiable and highly practical. The material acts like a mirror in one's life and once we understand how negative anger affects our relationships with others it brings about a strong desire to change our current course of living. *Mike Pratt Senior Pastor – Communion Chapel, San Antonio, Texas*

We have this in common, we are all human beings with positive and negative emotions. Love, joy and peace are positive emotions we enjoy. However, negative emotions such as blame, shame and guilt can seriously rob us of an enjoyable life. One emotion, anger, handled in a negative manner can quickly destroy contentment in our lives. This book gives six tools to win over negative anger. While these tools are not complicated in concept, they are extremely effective when put into practice. Any person dealing with negative anger should read this book, and continue to review the principles and concepts when needed. This book can be the catalyst to change a life impacted by the effects of negative anger into a life that is peaceful and productive. *Janet L. Hughes, Grant Writer, Instructional Designer*

Watching local or national news, walking city streets, driving on the highway at rush hour or shopping in malls gives the impression of an anger epidemic in America and in the world. There is a better way. *From Anger to Contentment* addresses the problems of anger in a very accessible manner The language is simple to understand and the methods are practical. The book is appropriate for use in classrooms, study groups, support groups and for personal growth. The methods are effective in personal relationships, in the workplace and even in international relations. *Karion Krieger, MDiv, DMin Anger Management Facilitator*

Sincere thanks and blessing to "Our Team"

Jay Burchfield and Renee Smith
Raymond Vela and Ben Freeman
George Walton and Cynthia Freeman
Sandee M. Johns and Lea Glisson
Jim Ryan and Texie Bohannan
and Troy LeBlanc,
and all other book contributors.

I, Frank Bohannan, am most grateful to the members of "Our Team," who gave their personal time and spirit-filled dedication to this unique ministry effort. Their professionalism and maturity provided the necessary prayer and hands-on support to complete this faithful higher power inspired task for the emotionally wounded living on the angry road around the world. Without their desire to be part of a helpful thing, this book would still be on our long to do list and may never have been accomplished for the benefit of an emotionally wounded world.

We hope this book will be a part of a peaceful revolution in an angry America and an angry world. Without spiritual insights and sincere tool application, this world will only become angrier, both outside and inside the higher power believing world.

CONTENTS

FOREWORD

Anger is an emotion we all experience, at some time in life. Unfortunately, anger can become a destructive force which can change the course of a life, in just a few minutes. Words uttered or actions taken under the influence of non-righteous anger can have devastating results.

We see anger in every part of our society. We observe anger in our workplaces, our schools and our families. Unfortunately, anger can even invade our churches. Our jails and prisons attest to the fact many individuals cannot control their anger emotion. Divorce courts and juvenile facilities also are clear illustrations that anger can be instrumental in breaking once loving relationships.

Throughout this book reference is made to a "higher power." The concept of a higher power has been used in successful twelve-step programs over the years. Many people of various faiths and traditions will identify their higher power as God. Others will simply identify their higher power as a feeling or force greater than themselves. No matter what definition is being used, being open to the concept of a higher power is a strong foundation for managing negative anger and other negative emotions.

This book is the result of helping over 35,000 people who have asked for help in managing and controlling their emotion of negative anger. The information in this book is more than just theory. It has been used successfully by real people, with genuine anger issues. Our earnest hope is this tried and true information you receive will be instrumental in a life changing experience.

INTRODUCTION

We are unique individuals in one way or another. Our personalities are different as well as many of our personal preferences. We differ in the type of entertainment we enjoy and the way we spend our leisure time. These differences extend into very personal areas of our lives, including our religious beliefs and the priority we place on our morals and values.

It is not surprising that humans cope with their emotions in various ways with varying degrees of success. We all seem to be rather proficient at handling our positive emotions such as joy, happiness and love. The difficulty comes in effectively ruling over negative emotions such as blame, shame, guilt and negative anger.

After more than twenty-two years of working with those who are experiencing or have experienced the negative effects of anger, we have developed six basic anger management tools. When used with purpose and conviction, these tools have proven to be highly effective in controlling and managing negative anger. The purpose of each tool is as follows:

	Tool	Purpose
1	The **S-T-O-P** word	Start controlling anger immediately
2	The Confident Persuasive Message	How to communicate when angry
3	The Anger Log	Personality study and mental picture of anger
4	Responsibility Model	Understanding the number one cause of anger
5	Reconciliation Process	Reconciling with yourself and others
6	High Way Journey	Knowing where you are now and determining where you are going

We are confident about our ability to provide a strong and effective program as outlined in this book. We cannot, however, provide a passion and sincere desire to achieve success. Spirituality now becomes essential. Call upon your higher power for the will, hunger and desire to change. Through the influences of your higher power, the results can be amazing.

TOOL ONE
THE S-T-O-P WORD

Every person experiences anger at some time in life. It's not a subject that is often used in polite conversation. Those whose lives have been negatively affected by negative anger are usually reluctant to discuss the subject. The truth is that the vast majority of people have had their lives impacted by anger, to some degree. The most common effect of anger is the destruction of relationships. This fact is plainly seen in our divorce rates and the dysfunctions that occur within our families. There is no magic wand to control and manage the negative anger emotion. If an individual sincerely wishes to start the process of managing his emotions, he must make this desire a high priority in his life. If that type of effort is made, there is no reason to doubt a successful result.

A good starting point is a general discussion about the anger emotion. An interesting fact about the anger emotion is that it is neither good nor evil. The anger emotion is neutral. We determine if we use the emotion in a positive or negative way. This indicates an interesting fact that all anger is not negative. There is such a thing as good anger. When we hear or see things that are obviously immoral or unjust, we should be angry. We should have the ability to distinguish right from wrong.

Another interesting fact is that many times anger starts defensively. Two people can be on the opposite sides of an issue. Each will try to defend his position. If there is no compromise in a person's thinking, the defensive position can lead to aggression and anger. When we discuss the **S-T-O-P** word later in this chapter, an important point will be made. Simply stated, one should try to see the opposite point of view, when there is a conflict of opinions. Over the years many people have confided that an angry event did not start with an aggressive attitude. It simply started with two different positions that elevated into aggression. It would be a perfect world if everyone could just

1

agree to disagree. Unfortunately, we do not live in a perfect world.

Responses to Anger

We all have three different responses to anger: physical, emotional and spiritual. Physical responses vary from person to person. We definitely know we are getting angry by the way our bodies react during the beginning of the anger process. Some of the physical responses are muscles tightening, blood pressure elevating, voice increasing in volume, heavy breathing or eyes dilating. These physical responses are a red flag warning that we are about to become angry. If you hear someone say, "I didn't know I was getting angry," that is a false statement. We all know when we are becoming angry because of our physical responses.

Emotional responses may include deep hurts, frustrations and anxiety. Most people have experienced some hurt and frustration in their lives as a result of negative anger. In some cases these emotional responses last for many years and in some cases for a lifetime. One of the best remedies for emotional hurts and frustrations is forgiveness. In a later chapter we will be discussing in depth the subject of forgiveness. This subject should be uppermost in the minds of everyone, and yet, it is one of the most difficult accomplishments for most people, regardless of their spiritual beliefs.

Spiritual responses help us see clearly, think positively, feel closer to our higher power, give us a more positive attitude and improve our behavior. They also help define happiness. The definition of happiness for most people seems to be just being content with the circumstances of their lives.

Fight or Flight Concept

In the general discussion of anger, perhaps there is no more important topic than the "fight or flight" concept. A great number of people believe the best way to handle an angry event is simply to walk away. In the short run, there really isn't anything wrong with this strategy. Walking away for a few minutes, an hour, or even a day or two may be helpful. However, one must also walk back or the anger issue may never be resolved. Rather than walk away, the situation may call on us to "fight." We don't mean physical fighting. What we do mean is being able to defend our position verbally and to confront the other person in an intelligent and assertive way. The reason most people use flight in anger is because they feel incapable of communicating when they are getting angry or when they are already angry. One example is an employee that is fired from his job because of inadequate training. Should he just walk away in anger? No. The better course is to fight for his job by asking for more time to improve his performance or seek additional training. A fuller discussion of how to speak assertively will be covered in Chapter 2.

Brain Chemistry

Have you ever asked yourself this question, "Why do I act or behave the way I do?" People who experience emotional difficulties with angry outbursts do wonder why they exhibit such behavior. Our moods and our emotions are controlled by our brain chemistry, which is conditioned by learned behavior. In order to gain an elementary knowledge of the brain chemistry process, please observe the following illustration.

ENERGY PATH

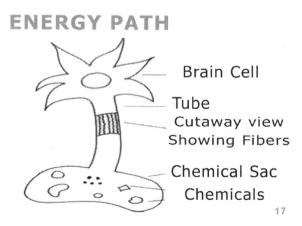

Brain Cell

Tube
Cutaway view
Showing Fibers

Chemical Sac

Chemicals

17

3

* Illustrations are numbered for use in classes.

This is not the illustration of an actual brain cell. This illustration looks like a leaning palm tree or a drooping daisy. It will, however, simplify the explanation of brain chemistry.

To begin the discussion of brain chemistry, we must recognize that there are three energies involved in this process. These three energies are mechanical energy, electrical energy and chemical energy. If someone makes a hurtful remark to you, he or she creates mechanical energies which are sound waves. These sound waves enter your ear and travel to your ear drums, causing vibrations. This vibration sends the sound waves to the brain. On the way to the brain these sound waves convert into electrical impulses. The electrical impulses enter the brain cell and proceed down the tube by way of fibers located in the cell tube. At the bottom of the tube is the chemical sac that contains various chemicals. These are the chemicals that produce our moods and our emotions. An astounding fact is that the electrical charges and chemicals move together through the brain cells at an estimated speed of 280 miles per hour. Here is a partial list of the chemicals and their functions:

CHEMICAL	FUNCTION
Adrenaline	Energy, Alertness
Endorphin	Pleasure, Enjoyment
Serotonin	Peaceful, REM Sleep
Dopamine	Reward, Euphoria
Epinephrine	Adrenaline increase
Norepinephrine	Anger, Righteous Anger
	Anger, Unrighteous Anger, Wrath, Fury, Rage

The next logical concern is how the electricity is directed to the various chemicals. We direct electrical paths through our learned behavior. For example, if a person's learned behavior is one of anger, the electrical charges will stimulate the adrenaline and norepinephrine. Learned behavior starts at a very early age and continues unaltered unless we change that behavior pattern. Changing our behavior does change our brain chemistry. That is why good anger management instruction or various twelve-step programs are successful. They change behavior which in turn changes brain chemistry.

At this point, a great question is "What makes you angry and why?" It is amazing that some people will answer that they really don't know why they get angry. That is not an acceptable answer. If you don't know why you are angry, you really have no reason to be angry.

S-T-O-P Word

We can now move to our first anger management tool which we call the "**S-T-O-P** Word." We have all seen a stop sign:

When you come to a corner with a stop sign while driving, the wise course of action is to stop. It is amazing that some of the consequences of running the stop sign could range from having a serious accident to receiving an unwanted traffic ticket. In anger management the thought is to stop the anger emotion when we first feel the physical, spiritual or emotional responses to anger. In other words stop the anger event before it gets a firm foothold on our emotions. The big question is, how this can be accomplished? Is it really possible to have a quick mental process that will bring the anger emotion under control before it gains power over behavior? The answer is a definite "Yes." When the responses of anger occur, you should use the stop word as an acronym as follows:

The "S" in the S-T-O-P Word means STOP. Have you ever heard or read anywhere that you have to do something when you feel the responses to anger? The answer is that you don't have to do anything. If you are sitting down or lying down, then stay down. If you are standing up, don't move and don't talk. This inactivity will bring down your metabolism and start giving you a sense of control. The period of time you stop depends on you and the situation, but it doesn't take long. Perhaps it will take 10 or 15 seconds or even 30 seconds. Look at your watch or clock. Thirty seconds can seem like a lifetime if you are not doing any activity.

The "T" in the S-T-O-P Word means THINK. What are you supposed to think about? The answer is to think about your behavior. What voices of anger are you hearing? Look at the voices of anger illustrations below:

Voices of *Anger*

- Childish Child – (me)
- Big Bully – (me)
- Critical Parent – (me)
- Mature Adult-Us with Higher Power

Unfortunately, most people think like a child when they become angry. Their thoughts include "I don't deserve to be treated this way," or "Why are you treating me this way?" Their thoughts become childlike in nature. They basically feel they are being disciplined like a child.

The second way immature people think when they are angry is like a bully. If you can remember bullies from your childhood, they don't actually like to fight, but they really enjoy bullying others. If someone can make you do something or react in some way using the tactics of a bully, he or she will continue to do so until you or someone else actually stands up to that type of behavior. Bully thinking only produces negative results.

The third way people think when they are angry is as a critical parent. They speak to another adult as if they were lecturing a child. Obviously, this will cause anger and resentment in others. The use of threats or rewards may be successful with children but not with adults.

How should we think when we first feel the physical, spiritual and emotional responses to anger? We should think as mature adults with our higher power. When we think in this manner, we ask ourselves, "What is the most responsible action we can take immediately?" That action may be to walk away for a while. The key words are "a while." Eventually we must return and address the anger issue, or it will never be resolved.

The third letter in the S-T-O-P Word is the "O", which stands for being OPEN. Be open to the other person's point of view. Actually listen to what the other person has to say. Have you ever stopped to think that the other person may be right? How would you know whether he or she has correct or incorrect thinking unless you actually listen? If you are listening to someone, give him your full attention; never try to multi-task when listening.

The last letter in the ST-O-P Word is the "P" which stands for the PROBLEM. For the angry person, the problem is the anger. As a comparison, use this thought: it is what an alcoholic does and says under the influence of alcohol that causes the problem. Likewise, it is what the angry person does and says under the influence of anger that causes the problem. So for the angry person, we can say that the real problem is the anger. We tend to deny this by playing mental games with ourselves. The first game is the blame game. It is always somebody else's fault that we are angry. This is the most common game people play, but the simple truth is other people are not the problem. They are simply the triggers because they trigger our anger. We will never run out of triggers; there will always be someone or something to trigger our anger. The trigger is not the real problem; the real problem is our anger and how we act on it.

Tool One - Teacher Story

Sometimes simple reasoning replaces thoughts and ideas that we believed would be difficult and complicated. Here is one such story.

I had a client who was a high school teacher with an unusual anger problem. He not only was a teacher, but also was the varsity coach for one of the school's athletic teams. In his personal life, his leisure time was spent playing golf and tennis. His anger problem seemed to be the exact opposite from what most people experience. He didn't become angry from the various pressures of his work. He did not show anger at students in the classroom when he became frustrated at their inability or lack of effort to learn. He didn't become angry at his team players who failed to execute after being coached properly. His anger came on the golf course and tennis court when he performed poorly. By his own admission, over a period of five or six years he had ruined numerous golf clubs by throwing them in a lake or hitting them against his golf cart. He had also ruined a few good tennis rackets with the same type of behavior. So the vast majority of his anger occurred when he should have been relaxing and having fun. New golf clubs and tennis rackets made his anger extremely expensive.

Tool One - Medal of Honor Story

Specialist Fifth Class Charles (Chuck) Hagemeister, as a 20-year-old medic assigned to an infantry platoon of the 1st Battalion, 5th Cavalry, 1st Cavalry Division (airmobile), won our nation's highest award for valor. He has a *"righteous anger"* story to share with us that took place in the Republic of Vietnam, on March 20, 1967.

His citation basically reads in the following manner. *"For conspicuous gallantry and intrepidity in action at the risk of his life above and beyond the call of duty, Specialist Charles Chris Hagemeister is awarded the Medal of Honor.*

While conducting combat operations against a hostile force, Sp5c. Hagemeister's platoon suddenly came under heavy attack from three sides by an enemy force. They were well concealed, in fortified positions and supported by machine guns and mortars. Seeing two of his comrades seriously wounded in the initial action, Sp5c. Hagemeister unhesitatingly, and with total disregard for his safety, raced through the deadly hail of enemy fire to provide them medical aid. Upon learning that the platoon leader and several other soldiers also had been wounded, Specialist Hagemeister continued to brave the withering enemy fire and crawled forward to render lifesaving treatment and to offer words of encouragement. Attempting to evacuate the seriously wounded soldiers, Sp5c. Hagemeister was taken under fire at close range by an enemy sniper.

Realizing that the lives of his fellow soldiers depended on his actions, Sp5c. Hagemeister seized a rifle from a fallen comrade, killed the sniper, three other enemy soldiers who were attempting to encircle his position, and silenced an enemy machine gun that covered the area with deadly fire. Unable to remove the wounded to a less exposed location and aware of the enemy's efforts to isolate his unit, he dashed through the fusillade of fire to secure help from a nearby platoon. Returning with help, he placed men in positions to cover his advance as he moved to evacuate the wounded forward of his location. These efforts successfully completed, he then moved to the other flank and evacuated additional wounded men despite the fact that his every move drew fire from the enemy.

Specialist Hagemeister's repeated heroic and selfless actions at the risk of his life, saved the lives of many of his comrades and inspired their actions in repelling the enemy assault. Sp5c. Hagemeister's indomitable courage was in the highest traditions of the U.S. Armed Forces and reflects great credit upon himself."

Comment Added: Later, as a Lieutenant Colonel working for one of our retired Army officer anger management facilitators, Chuck added the following insight. During the initial chaos and terror of the ambush, he steadfastly did what he was trained to do – save lives. But when the sniper intentionally wounded him, clearly identified as a medic, and fired at those he was trying to save, he said, "That's when I got angry!" We hope this is a beautiful illustration of the difference between righteous anger and unrighteous anger. What a young, modern day hero!

Tool One - Inmate Bacon Story

I was teaching a small group of inmates the importance of using the stop word as quickly as possible. When I returned to teach the following week, I asked the inmates if they had practiced what they learned about the stop word. One inmate said, "Absolutely. It saved my bacon." "What do you mean, it saved your bacon?" I asked. He responded by telling me his cellie (two inmates are housed in a small two person cell at night while they sleep) woke up in the middle of the night having withdrawal pains from using cocaine. His cellie began to beat on him but our student client refused to fight back and used his stop word – **S-T-O-P**. Instead of fighting, he called for the nearby guard and the cellie was removed and taken to lockdown. Had our student responded in his usual manner, he would have joined his cellie in lockdown for fighting. Our student had previously been in lockdown two times previously. More than likely, a third trip to lockdown would have resulted in additional time on his sentence. The use of this word **S-T-O-P** allowed this inmate to stay in control of his anger and not return to lockdown. In other words, as he said in class, "it saved my bacon." If this can work for an incarcerated high school dropout, it can work for you.

One of the statements that we make in Tool 1 of our course is "Balance is found when anger is linked to a reasonable issue and communicated in the proper manner." When my client read this statement his comment was "WOW." He then proceeded to tell me that a light just turned on in his mind. The throwing of golf clubs and the ruining of tennis rackets was not reasonable behavior. It is amazing to me that this was not obvious to him before he was introduced to that statement. Therefore, in using the **S-T-O-P** word he said that the "T" for him was obvious. Just that one simple thought process became a major factor in his vastly improved behavior.

Blame Game

- ANGER JUSTIFICATION

- QUESTION: WHO IS IN CONTROL?

- SELF-CONTROL IS CRITICAL

In addition to the blame game many people will use anger justification. We will tell others about our anger and hope they will agree we should be angry about whatever occurred. Anger justification will help relieve any guilt feelings that we have about our anger. The real question we face with the anger emotion is, who is in control? There is an indisputable fact that you cannot be in control of your anger, and out of control with your anger, at the same time. It's either one or the other, and self-control is absolutely critical. We should all realize that self-control is just as important as love, joy, peace and other positive feelings and positive emotions.

Identifying Anger Sources

We all have experienced negative anger in our lives, and it would seem that the causes or the sources of anger come from many different places and many different events in our lives. In order to simplify our thinking, we can divide the sources of anger into three major categories. We will discuss each of these sources; however, the effect on the individual will be the same.

The **first** source of anger is <u>maintaining our personal worth</u>. If a person lives in a condescending atmosphere at home or at work, anger is very likely to occur. We all think that our ideas and our opinions have some value. When no one listens to us or dismisses what we think or what we feel, we start to question our personal worth. Each of us has thoughts, ideas and opinions that have value from time to time. The question is, is anyone interested in hearing what we are trying to communicate, or do they simply dismiss what we have to say?

The **second** source of anger is <u>protecting critical needs</u>. Critical needs vary from person to person. Here are a few good examples: Most people like the company of others in their lives. Others require quiet time alone, and for them that is an essential need. Some people enjoy a great amount of conversation while others are quiet types who do not require much verbal communication. Some people enjoy a great amount of human touch and love to be kissed and hugged, while others require very little physical contact. When individuals receive more or less than they desire, anger can occur.

The **third** source of anger is <u>upholding our basic beliefs</u>. We all have some important beliefs in our lives. These include strong feelings about faith and religion, and politics and social issues. Confronting an individual in any of these areas can create anger. When opposite views occur in our convictions, we can expect others to challenge some of our ideas. Compromising deep and basic convictions is a difficult process and can result in substantially angry attitudes.

These anger sources will all produce the same effect, to one degree or another. The effect will be deep hurts, deep frustration, deep insecurity or anxiety. Over the years in our classes we ask our students how many have experienced a deep hurt in their lives. It seems that the response is always overwhelming, because most will indicate that they have had such an experience.

In addition to the hurts caused by negative anger, there are some other unwanted results. The first is self-anger. We become angry at ourselves because we feel incapable of handling the hurts we have experienced. Self-anger triggers additional unwanted emotions such as self-guilt, blame and shame. Numerous personal losses can occur as a result of anger. These could include loss of a marriage, loss of a relationship with children, loss of a job, or in some cases even the loss of a profession. Relationships can be easily damaged, and may be extremely difficult to restore. Perhaps one of the most tragic results may be the loss of spirituality or at least a tarnish of spirituality to one degree or another.

None of the effects and results of anger we have discussed are positive. In reality, some individuals reach the lowest point in their life, and make a life changing decision not to accept emotional defeat. It is at the very bottom they find a renewed spark of faith and determination through their higher power to make significant changes in thinking and behavior.

I personally experienced a very deep hurt at a young age. I was born and raised in a happy and religious home. I was active in school activities and played high school sports, which I enjoyed very much. My father was a doctor of medicine and stayed extremely busy in his office, making house calls and being at the hospital. My mother was the typical housewife. I had a very close relationship with my mother. Both my sister and I loved our parents. A few months after I graduated from high school, my mother had a major stroke and passed away. Although she had suffered from high blood pressure, I never believed that anything of that nature would happen to me. I can remember feeling great loss and sorrow, and I certainly felt I had reached the lowest point in my life.

Less than two years later, we found that my father had developed cancer. This was not a slow growing cancer and it had already progressed to his internal organs. When this cancer was discovered, his doctors told me he had approximately six months to live. In reality he lived for only 91 days. My sister had married and moved across the country and had a new baby, so she was not there to share that experience with me. Both sets of grandparents were deceased and now my parents were also deceased. My mother was an only child so there were no aunts or uncles on that side of the family.

My dad had two brothers, both of whom were deceased. One had never married and the other had been married and divorced and had one son, whom I had never met. At that point in my life I felt completely alone. In fact, I was almost completely alone and lonely. My frustration became anger, and in my own mind, I became angry at everyone. As I saw so many of my friends with their families intact, I had deep feelings of hurt and frustration because I was now alone. I really don't believe it would be unusual under those circumstances for a young man to feel all the emotions that I felt, or to be angry and eliminate any thought of a higher power that could restore the happiness in my life. It would be a wonderful story if I could honestly relate that I dismissed the anger in a short period of time. However, that is not what occurred. I felt deep resentment for a number of years. Slowly, I started to realize how fortunate I had been to have the parents that I had for those years. Even today I see so many young people that come from dysfunctional situations and were not given the basic love and advantages that my parents were able to provide me. My anger slowly faded and the emotion of anger was replaced with the emotion of gratitude. In reality I used the **S-T-O-P** word but it was a process that developed over time. Today when I speak to individuals or classes, I can speak with authority because I have experienced their emotions.

Tool One - Glass of Wine Story

A well-spoken man called one day and asked if he could come in and discuss his anger issues. When he arrived, my first impression was of a finely dressed, professional looking man. Behind closed doors, he immediately said he needed some help with his anger. I concluded from his initial intake information that he was a practicing doctor who was well respected in the area. I started to explain the six tools in our program, but he stopped me when I shared the importance of using the first tool: our stop word **S-T-O-P**. Although I did not question him, he told me he needed that tool right now. The previous week, he and his wife had argued at the dinner table one evening, while they were both having a glass of wine. In anger, he knocked the crystal glass of wine on the floor. Afterward, he proceeded to clean it up with the hair of his wife while it was still on her head. He explained to me this was not the first time his anger had propelled him to react physically toward his wife and children. Once we got into the program, he was able to incorporate the use of this elementary tool and control his anger-provoked behavior more successfully. Several weeks later, when his wife started the program, she said this small **S-T-O-P** word had drastically improved their relationship. It can improve the relationship with your loved ones too, if you will use it.

Summary

When anger becomes a real problem in a person's life, there are numerous helps that are available. These range from professional help by psychiatrists and psychologists, to good anger management programs. Spiritual help is available by invoking our higher power. In addition, help and support are available from our family and friends. Help can even come from a stranger, if he or she happens to say the right thing at the right time.

The real question is not whether there is ready and willing help available, but does the individual want to be helped. No sources of help have a magic wand that will eliminate negative emotions. There must be a hunger, a strong will and a total desire to be helped. Without that type of desire, failure is almost assured. Managing and controlling negative emotions is not a part time job. We must be fully employed in the process. This is where our spirituality will play a major role. Look to your higher power for strength.

TOOL ONE TEST

Everyone remembers the days when they were going to school. Probably, almost 100% would agree that one of the most dreaded activities was the famous "Pop Quiz." We have a short test or quiz about our first tool. This is just a quick evaluation to measure your understanding of the material that was presented. The answers are at the end of the book. If you miss a question, go back and re-read the material in a timely manner so that the principle or concept is firmly established in your mind.

1. Our emotion of anger always starts in our minds as a:
    A. Good emotion
    B. Bad emotion
    C. Neither good nor bad emotion, but a neutral emotion
    D. One emotion that solely depends on the person and their relationship

2. In this anger management program, there are three responses to anger:
    A. Emotional, physical and intellectual
    B. Physical, spiritual and emotional
    C. Chemical, intellectual and mechanical
    D. Social, physical and motivational

3. The three active energies of anger in our heads and our brains are:
    A. Mechanical, electrical and chemical
    B. Spiritual, emotional and electrical
    C. Chemical, thermoelectric and heat
    D. Mechanical, higher power and electrical

4. The root causes of our anger come from trying to preserve which three areas of our life:

A. Family worth, critical needs and basic wants

B. Financial worth, critical needs and basic beliefs

C. Worldly worth, critical expectations and beliefs

D. Personal worth, critical needs and basic beliefs

5. The anger S-T-O-P word is most helpful and stands for four words:

A. Stand, Try, Oppose and Protect

B. Start, Tunnel, Open and Prevent

C. Stay, Turn, Oppress and Prepare

D. Stop, Think, Open and Problem

6. The non-audible voices of anger that may motivate people to respond are:

A. Childish creditor, big bald head, critical person or immature adult

B. Childish child, big bully, critical parent or mature adult

C. Childish chicken, big blamer, critical person or mature manager

D. Childish chum, big baby, critical parent or immature mother/father

7. All of the four letters in the S-T-O-P word are important, but the most important or most insightful letter is "P: Problem" for the following reason:

A. We all must live with bad anger Problems in mature relationships

B. The Problem of bad anger is always right justified

C. Anger is our Problem and it can't be controlled by what triggers us

D. The anger Problem is a curse from my parents or grandparents

8. The Blame Game is played by most angry people. When we play the game:

A. We are in total control of our angry behavior

B. We are trying to justify our bad anger behavior

C. We really understand that self-control is critical

D. We are in complete agreement with our spiritual higher power

9. The chemical most related to the anger emotion is

A. Adrenaline

B. Endorphin

C. Serotonin

D. Norepinephrine

10. The critical point of this first anger management tool follows: "This S-T-O-P word must be central to all anger management activity in your life."

A. True

B. False

TOOL TWO
CONFIDENT PERSUASIVE MESSAGE

In beginning a discussion of how to control our speech when we feel the physical, spiritual and emotional responses to the negative anger emotion, we must realize that learned behavior plays an important role. Most psychologists will agree that at least 70% to 80% of all behavior is learned behavior. From a very early age, we start the learned behavior process. We all learned behavior, whether it was positive, neutral or negative, from others. Certainly people such as our parents, our teachers and our friends had an influence on our learned behavior.

The experiences we have in our lives will help shape our behavior. The positive or negative experiences we have as young children can leave lasting impressions. As we recall these experiences and events, we also recall the emotions created by those experiences. We can learn the wrong ABCs of anger, but we can also relearn the right or correct ABCs of anger.

Learned Behavior

- Mis-learned ABCs of anger (wrong)
  - A = Anger should be normally acceptable
  - B = Blame game playing is acceptable
  - C = Criticism/sarcasm is acceptable
- Re-learned ABCs of anger (right)
  - A = Abstain from negative anger behaviors
  - B = Believe in and use spiritual principles
  - C = Communicate (low volume & sweet tone)

Cycles of Addiction

Over the years we have found, to our surprise, that most of

our students and clients accept the fact that emotions, as well as physical substances, can become addictive. Everyone accepts the fact that alcohol, drugs, food, etc. can become addictive. Unfortunately, we see far too much of the results of these addictions in our society. An addiction to an emotion would include emotions such as negative anger, blame, shame and guilt. In order to understand these addictions, we must realize that addictions, whether physical or emotional, do cycle. We will illustrate these cycles.

The first cycle which is illustrated is the physical cycle of addiction:

The Cycle of Addiction
(Behavioral Problem)

RECOVERY

SEEK HELP   STRONG FEELINGS

SOLEMN RESOLVES   REMEMBERED PLEASURES

EMERGE REMORSEFUL   TELLING SELF LIES AND BELIEVING THEM

CRISIS   USE

BINGE

Please note that an addiction is definitely a behavioral problem. Since individuals are not engaged in their addictive behavior every minute of the day, they technically go through a period of recovery. The addict then starts to have strong feelings because he remembers the pleasure he experienced. The next step in the cycle is telling lies, and believing them. The most common lies are "this is the last time," and "I can quit permanently any time I choose." The addict will then use the physical substance and will generally overuse or binge, as the addictions becomes more intense. This overuse generally will lead to some type of crisis for which the addict will be remorseful. This remorse will lead to making solemn resolves or promises to stop the addiction and seek help from some source. This help could come from a professional counselor, a coach, a pastor, a family member, or a friend. The addict may again go through a period of recovery. The problem is that they again will feel the strong feelings, and the cycle will repeat itself time and time again. The emotional cycle of addiction is a mind-body-behavioral problem. Please observe the following illustration:

The Cycle of Anger Addiction
(Mind-Body Behavioral Problem)

RECOVERY

SEEKS HELP   STRONG FEELINGS
                          MISMANAGEMENT

SOLEMN   REMEMBERED *FEELINGS*
RESOLVES   PAST HURTS

EMERGE   TELLING SELF LIES
REMORSEFUL   AND BELIEVING THEM

CRISIS   USE

BINGE

*OBESSIVE THINKING + COMPULSIVE BEHAVIOR = **AN ADDICTION***

This emotional cycle is the same as the physical cycle in it is basic concept, but different in the first five cycle events. For our discussion we will use a person addicted to the anger emotion. Obviously, this addict will not be angry every moment of every day, however, when an angry event or situation occurs that triggers their anger emotion, the strong feelings will occur. These will be feelings of mismanagement, such as blaming others for their anger. They may also mismanage the emotion by trying to continually justify their angry behavior. The person will then remember past feelings. These will not be feelings of pleasure, but feelings of past hurts. Next, the emotional addicts will tell themselves lies, such as the blame game or trying to justify their anger. Predictably, our addict will not use any non-anger tools such as the **S-T-O-P** word or the confident persuasive message. As the addicts advance in the anger emotion, they will binge on the anger by revisiting the harmful anger of the past. This binging will easily lead to a crisis. The crisis of anger can include court, arrest, jail, loss of employment, loss of family or loss of a valued friend. The addict will then emerge from the anger event remorseful and make solemn resolves and promises never to be as angry again. At this point, many addicts seek help from professional counselors, coaches, pastor, family or friends. Some addicts can then experience some measure of recovery, but in the future will again recall the same strong feelings and the cycle begins again.

At this point, three important facts must be discussed. The first concerns the true definition of an addiction. If a person has obsessive thinking followed by compulsive behavior, they have developed an addiction. This is true whether it is a physical substance or an emotional thought. The second fact is that the most effective way to stop a cycle of any addiction is to realize that addictions must be stopped at the very beginning of the cycle. Therefore, the most effective way to stop an addiction from cycling and cycling again is to stop it at the strong feeling point. The further an addict advances in the cycle, the more difficult it becomes to stop the cycle. If an addict reaches a point where he is lying to himself, the chances of stopping the cycle are extremely remote.

The third fact is that most recovering addicts will agree that recognizing and relying on their higher power was of significant help in their journey through their addiction. The recognition of a higher power concept has been one of the most significant principles of successful twelve-step programs. If the higher power recognition has had a life-changing effect on others, it should warrant careful consideration and acceptance. We have served over 35,000 clients in the area of anger and stress management, and our observation has been that those clients that have a higher power relationship have reached a much higher rate of achievement and success. Do not ignore this vital concept.

Confident Persuasive Message

Most people have difficulty communicating when they are angry. We hear many stories of yelling, screaming and cursing when the responses to the emotion of anger first appear. Therefore, a huge part of anger management is knowing how to speak during those angry events. In order to accomplish this goal, we must have a formula or message that will accomplish our purpose.

The first thought that must be in our mind is that we want to be honest and say exactly what we mean and mean exactly what we say. In order to succeed, we must be able to speak in a confident and persuasive manner. Our suggestion is to master the use of an anger management tool which is simply called the "Confident Persuasive Message." This is a three-part message that will lead to meaningful and safe dialogue. However, before we discuss the actual three-part message a more general discussion of how anger works should be helpful.

Every person has two minds. We have a conscious mind and a subconscious mind. In our conscious mind we are all aware of the events around us each day. The subconscious mind is very different because we can't see what is in it. For our purposes we will call our subconscious mind a "backpack." Most everyone at one time or another has worn a backpack. Some of the common characteristics of a backpack are as follows:

- We can't see what is in the backpack
- We spend our lives stuffing events in our backpack
- Some of these events in the backpack are long forgotten
- We carry many emotions in our backpack

Some of the good emotions we carry in the backpack are the emotions of joy, happiness, peace, contentment, love and fulfillment. A few of the bad emotions in the backpack are pain, confusion, trauma, shame, guilt, resentment and misery. The important point to grasp is that when we speak in anger, we are speaking from our emotions. Some of these angry events are conscious events because they are happening now. However, some of these angry events have had their origin in the past and are recalled by our subconscious mind. Whatever the source of the anger, how we communicate becomes vitally important.

The first and primary thought in proper communication is to not use foul or abusive language. Let everything you say be positive and encouraging to those that hear you. Foul and abusive language will only inflame the emotions of those that hear that language. There are several other extremely important principles and concepts to master the art of controlling angry communication. The most asked question our facilitators encounter is whether a person should just walk away from an angry situation, or stay and fight. The common language is whether a person should fight or flee. Obviously, there is nothing wrong with walking away for a short time. However, the problem is that most people who walk away, don't walk back. If a person doesn't walk back, the anger event will never be brought to a conclusion. When we do walk back, we should not want to fight. Our higher power has given us a desirable third option. We can actually resolve our differences by talking things out with others if people in the relationship care about each other. This is important because minor harmful differences tend to grow larger. Another important thought is that our behavior should be chosen, not driven by our anger. Our words should be selected and not driven by anger. Cursing words are triggering words.

We must use the confident and persuasive message in our conversations that are disruptive and tense and could lead to negative angry and aggressive behavior. This message must be sent with a goal to change the other person's specific harmful behavior. We can't change another person, but we can try to change their behavior to one extent or another. Our message says you are intruding on my space (any space.) This could be your political, religious space or any other space for which you have deep convictions. Remember the confident persuasive message is characterized by firmness, but without domination (not submissive or aggressive.) This message should lead to a meaningful and safe dialogue.

CONFIDENT PERSUASIVE
MESSAGE FORMULA

I feel_____

_____

_____

(State Your Feelings)

The first part of this message is to state your real feelings. If you are angry, state that you are angry. If you are frustrated, irritated or anxious, state those exact feelings. If you don't state your real feelings, how will the other person know? The second part of this message is to state that you have those feelings when certain situations, events or discussions occur. One important item in this portion of the message is to avoid the word "you" as you state the second part of the message. If you state "when you" the other person will immediately feel uncomfortable and defensive. They will feel they are in the witness box and you are the prosecutor. Just simply state how you feel when certain events or situations occur or reoccur. Finally, you must tell the other person why you feel the way you feel. In other words, you have to have a "because." An example of this message would be

CONFIDENT PERSUASIVE
MESSAGE

■ EXAMPLE:
 ▷ I feel irritated and frustrated
   (State your real FEELINGS)
 ▷ When food and dishes are left on the table after breakfast
   (State their BEHAVIOR, NOT the person)
 ▷ Because we had agreed, if I prepared the meal, I would get help
   clearing the table.
   (State real negative EFFECT on your life)

26

as follows:

The main concept of this message is to be sure to focus on the other person's behavior, not on them as an individual. Express the message with the following:

- Love, respect
- Humility
- Compassion
- Consistency

After using this message, continuing dialogue is very important. In the follow-up conversation, the most vital rule is to stay on the topic. Do not wander away from the subject that is being discussed. If focus is not maintained, the effect of the message will be lost. An illustration of the principles for a safe dialogue is as follows:

PRINCIPLES FOR SAFE DIALOGUE
(Immediately After Persuasive Message

MESSAGE

AGREE TO ACTION

LISTEN TO THEIR
VIEWS/OPTIONS

CLEARLY STATE
OPTIONS

TOPIC

COMPLETELY HONEST

NO INAPPROPRIATE
LANGUAGE

BE RESPECTFUL

DESCRIBE A TENTATIVE GOAL
(I WOULD LIKE...) NOTE: DIFFICULT WITHOUT HIGHER POWER

As can be observed from the illustration, in addition to staying on the topic, there must be complete honesty. Make sure no inappropriate words are used. Curse words would be considered inappropriate. Be as respectful as possible and describe a tentative goal. The goal should be to make every effort to understand the other person's thinking or position on the subject. Tell the other person you would really like to know why they feel the way they do on any particular issue. A great statement would be, "I really would like to understand why you feel the way you do; please help me understand." Another good statement would be, "I would really like for you to understand exactly why I feel the way I do." These are non-threatening statements and show a real interest and concern for the other person's feelings. At this point, clearly state any options that you may have and listen to any alternative views or options the other person may offer. Once this point has been reached, move to action should be taken. The move to action should include such points as where, when, how and for what period of time the action should occur.

Good communication skills are vitally important in maintaining good relationships. Most individuals that experience difficulty in communicating effectively with others have no guide track or pathway to follow. The confident persuasive message, together with the principles for safe dialogue, will provide the necessary pathway to sound and effective verbal communications. One parting comment before we close this tool number two: please give your loved one more positive three-part confident persuasive messages. We all need to be congratulated from time to time. Look for things to build up your partner with a positive message.

TOOL TWO TEST

1.   Experiences during our childhood leave lasting impressions. When we recall the event, we also recall the:

   A.   Exact season of that year: winter, summer, spring or fall

   B.   Exact age we were when that good or bad experience occurred

   C.   Exact emotion (s) attached to the specific recalled event (s)

   D.   Exact hour of the day or night when the recalled event occurred

2.   Based on expert research and opinions, what percentage of our behavior is learned

   A.   90-110%

   B.   80-90%

   C.   70-80%

   D.   40-60%

3.   An anger management professional believes that most angry people have learned the wrong "ABC's" of good anger management procedures. The right "ABC's" of good anger management are:

   A.   Abstain from bad or negative behavior, believe in spiritual principles and communicate in low volume and sweet tone

   B.   Abstain from negative behavior, believe in self-preservation and communicate in a submissive way

   C.   Abstain from brash behavior, believe in self pride and count your many blessings while naming them one by one

   D.   Attack bad behavior with aggression, believe in

others over self and comment with criticism and sarcasm toward others

4. **The anger addiction cycle departs from recovery. If one is addicted to anger, what would they most likely remember at cycle point two?**

    A.   Remembered strong pleasures

    B.   Remembered strong feelings

    C.   Remembered strong energies

    D.   Remembered strong results

5. **When understanding how anger works, we know that we attach emotions to the past events in our lives. Where are the emotions stored in our body?**

    A.   Hearts

    B.   Conscious minds

    C.   Souls or spirits

    D.   Subconscious minds

6. **The Confident Persuasive Message has no pre-conceived solution, but it will/should lead to meaningful, safe dialogue with the other person.**

    A.   True

    B.   False

7. **The Confident Persuasive Message has the following starting parts to it:**

    A.   I believe, what, and whatever

    B.   I feel, when, and because

    C.   I know, where, and therefore

    D.   I think, why, and why not

8. **The important keys to a positive Confident Persuasive Message follow:**

    A.   Focus on the minor result, express in anger and forget about the future

    B.   Focus on others' thoughts, express in humility and

no positive messages

C.   Focus on motives, express in actions and many more negative messages

D.   Focus on others' behavior, express in love and give more positive messages

9.   After we share the Confident Persuasive Message with our loved ones, we should then follow up with a meaningful conversation using these principles:

A.   Focus on other like couples you both know and copy their behaviors

B.   Make the other person apologize and be abrasive

C.   Stay in good dialogue and move to positive agreeable actions

D.   Be prepared to move to silence or slight violence soon

10.   The most powerful negative or positive Confident Persuasive Message is one given:

A.   Somewhat submissively

B.   Assertively

C.   Somewhat aggressively

D.   Really aggressively

TOOL THREE
The Anger Log

The purpose of the anger log is to create a mental picture of anger. This is accomplished by answering questions pertaining to any particular anger event we have experienced. Remember when you were a child and connected the dots that slowly developed into a picture? The questions on the anger log are the dots. Our honest answers develop the mental picture of our anger. If we are displeased with our anger picture, necessary changes in our behavior become a necessity. We have a wonderful starting point for the anger log from the **S-T-O-P** word in Tool 1, and the Confident Persuasive Message described in Tool 2.

In starting this discussion, the first step is to examine the following anger log. Please read the questions carefully. Each question has a specific purpose and must be answered honestly for the log to give you a clear mental picture of your anger. The answers usually only require a few words, and for some just circle your response. The entire anger log should be completed in a short period of time. Look at the following anger log and carefully study the questions.

ANGER LOG

A. What led up to my anger?

_____

_____

B. Where was I when I felt the emotion of anger--no matter how small the emotion?

_____

_____

C. What pre-anger emotion (s) was I feeling (impatience, irritation, frustration, hurt etc.?)

_____

_____

D. What was I doing at the time of my anger (watching TV, texting, etc.?)

_____

_____

E. My physical response to my anger was (adrenaline, muscles, heart rate, breathing, etc.)

_____

_____

F. How successful was I in using the **S-T-O-P** word?

_____

_____

G. I usually am angry when I am with this person.
YES   NO   (CIRCLE ONE)

H. Is this person in authority or close to me?
YES   NO   (CIRCLE ONE)

I. Which voice was heard mostly during this anger event?

_____

_____

(Childish Child, or Big Bully, or Critical Parent, or Mature Adult)

J. What mismanagement strategy or strategies did I use in this event?
    (CIRCLE ALL USED)
    (Concealer, Self-absorber, Pretender or Exploder)

K. What misapplied method (s) did I use to support my strategy (s)?
    (CIRCLE ALL USED)
    (Downsize it, Postpone it, Weaken it, Transfer it, or Exclude it)

L. Did I learn anything from this anger event?
    YES   NO   (CIRCLE ONE)

M. If yes to the above question L, what did I learn?

_____

_____

_____

_____

_____

_____

In looking at the above anger log, the questions from letters "A" through "F" should be easily answered using the information from Tool 1 and Tool 2. The next two questions, letters "G" and "H" concern people with whom we have some relationship. The question of usually being angry with a particular person is interesting. Many times we are angry at the people who are the closest to us. This includes family members, co-workers, and friends. The reason is that they simply **are** the closest to us. We see and interact with them more on a regular basis. Over the years we have seen a great amount of anger between family members. Countless times we have heard husbands or wives say that they still "love" their spouse, but they don't "like" them because of their negative anger. The closer we are to a person, the more we observe their moods, emotions and behaviors. We must remember, however, that they are observing our characteristics also. No person has a perfect set of emotions. A well-known speaker once jokingly stated, "What a wonderful world this would be if everyone in this world was just like me." The central theme in this area is that we must show extra love, respect and understanding to those nearest and dearest to us.

As a close follow-up the next question asks if those in authority are the source of our anger. This includes our employers, public officials or any other persons that can impact our lives. The following is an interesting story about a young man who found the source of his anger was focused on female authority figures.

Tool Three - Female Boss Story

I was teaching anger management in our county jail, and the inmates were doing anger logs on a regular basis. When one inmate got to the question of authority as described in letter "H," he said the light came on. He had lost three jobs in a row prior to his arrest. In jail he was put in "lock-down" or segregation apart from the other inmates for short periods of time. This segregation occurred three times within a period of one month. When this young man answered the question as to his anger being directed at a person in authority, he stated that all three jobs were lost because of confrontations with his boss. In each case his boss was a female. Then as he was serving his sentence in jail, he was put in segregation because he questioned the authority of an officer. Each time the officer was a female. It became obvious that he could not accept authority from a female. He had no idea this was a real problem until he actually answered the question on the anger log honestly, and reflected on the fact that he had a significant problem with female authority. In other words, he started to connect the dots.

This story illustrates that once this inmate completed the anger log, he actually saw the source of much of his anger. He began to see the mental picture of his anger. These pictures were of previous employers and the jail officers which all just happened to be female. He really got the whole picture.

Now, we move to the anger log questions "J" and "H" which concern our strategies and methods of controlling our negative anger. These topics must start with a beginning discussion of personality. We can group personality types into three major categories. These three categories are submissive, assertive or aggressive. Each of these personality types has its own behavior style. The following are a few characteristics of each style.

First is the **submissive behavior style**:
- Lets others take advantage of him
- Ignores his own needs and wants
- Has a difficult time telling others "No"
- Is mostly passive, not very assertive

The second is the **assertive behavioral style:**

- Uses good communication skills (the Confident Persuasive Message in Tool 2)
- Speaks his own mind without putting others down
- Gives consideration to other people's feelings and points of view
- Tries to find each day enjoyable with good relationships with others

The third is the **aggressive behavior style:**
- Tends to be the bully and threatening type
- Dominates friends and family
- Can be abusive and rude
- Has a "my way or the highway" attitude

All of these behavioral styles do experience anger, from time to time. All three types can mismanage their anger emotion. This leads to a discussion of the four basic types of strategies for mismanaging anger. The strategies are as follows:

A. **Concealer** – This is the person who buries his anger. This individual may even think that all anger is wrong. The result is a great amount of stress which  can result in more serious physical and mental problems in the long term.

B. **Self-absorber** - This is the person who turns his anger inward and mostly blames himself with negative self-talk and thoughts.

C. **Pretender** – This person will rarely take responsibility for his own anger. Typically, after an anger event, he will claim not to have been angry. He will ask not to be taken seriously and may even joke about his anger. A typical statement of an under-hander would be, "You know I didn't really mean that, don't you?"

D. **Exploder** – Exploders can get out of control quickly. It is estimated that approximately 80% of exploding results from mental fatigue or the excessive use of alcohol. Exploders have a difficult time controlling what they say and their physical actions.

Tool Three - No Fun Story

A gentleman called one day and stated that he had been referred by a pastor. We made an appointment for him to come to our office, fill out our Intake Form and discuss his anger issues. When he arrived he appeared to be about six feet tall and in wonderful physical shape. He worked in the law enforcement arm of the Federal Government and had been educated at one of our military academies. While filling out our Intake Form he sat in an upright, rigid position and had a stern look on his face.

After completing the form, we moved into my private office and sat at a small table. Again I noticed he sat in a rigid position and his facial expression had not changed. I quickly glanced over his Intake Form and decided to ask him a question I am sure he did not expect. The question was "What do you do to have some fun?" Remarkably, he got up and moved his chair to my side of the table. In a very loud voice he said "Fun, did you say fun?" I assured him that that was my question and he responded in a very loud voice "I don't have any fun, what do you think life is, fun?"

This man was constantly on the verge of exploding with anger. It was also apparent that he had a severe case of mental fatigue. We point out rather forcefully in this third tool of our program that emotional explosions result from the overuse of alcohol and mental fatigue. This man's reactions are typical of many people that we see today. This is a complicated and fast-moving world which is causing mental fatigue for many people. One of the simple but effective answers for mental fatigue is simply to have some fun. Do what you enjoy doing and do it often.

Although this is not an exact science, those with submissive behavior will tend to conceal their anger or absorb themselves. Those with assertive behavior will tend to absorb or pretend their anger is not real. Those with aggressive behavior will tend to pretend their anger is not real or explode. The illustration below uses arrows to describe tendencies of mismanaged strategies.

BEHAVIOR CONTINUUM & MISMANAGED STRATEGIES

In addition to the four main strategies for expressing anger, there are five lesser strategies or supporting methods for handling our anger:

    A. Downsize it – making the anger event or situation seem to be much less than the obvious, which may take years of conditioning.

B. Postpone it – procrastinating by delaying the response to anger.

C. Weaken it - being less objective about the anger event. Anger is felt but is immediately watered down.

D. Transfer it – removing anger from one person, place or thing and putting it on a safer or less threatening person, place or thing. You can become angry for no apparent reason.

E. Exclude it – refusing to discuss the anger situation or event. Usually this involves being silent or simply walking away and refusing to communicate.

Any of these methods will only prolong anger and in some cases completely destroy a relationship. When these methods are adopted, the anger in the "backpack" (or our subconscious mind) will continue to grow. This will result in the person's being less capable of handling an angry situation or event.

The last two questions "L" and "M" are designed to measure your progress in seeing a mental picture of yourself, when experiencing an anger event. Also, you will discover if you are actually learning from the anger event. Hopefully, your response to each question is positive. The anger tools discussed in this book are the same as any other tools. They will be of great help only if they are used. The anger log is an excellent tool, as are the other tools, and should be used as an important activity in managing negative anger. The more the anger log is used, the more clearly you will see a real mental picture of your anger.

Please turn back to the anger log illustration, page 33, and mentally, or on a separate piece of paper, give your own answers to an anger event you have experienced in the past. Be honest with your answers and hopefully you will connect the dots and start to see in your own mind the picture of that event. We don't like to see ourselves in negative situations. If the picture you create in your own mind is not satisfactory, that is a warning sign that the anger management tools need to be put to use.

Tool Three - Like Father, Like Son Story

In class we routinely ask students how they and their spouses, or significant others, attempt to resolve conflicts. One man in his late twenties said he only knew one way to resolve a conflict with his live-in girlfriend, and that was the reason he was doing the anger management course. In other words, it was his way or the highway. When he wanted to make a decision that affected the family, he would routinely tell his partner what they were going to do, and how they were going to do it. If she did not immediately comply, he would raise his voice and curse at her. If he did not get his way he would explode, and if that was unsuccessful, he would become violent. When I asked him why he used that method to address a conflict, he had a very simple answer: that is how my mother and father resolved their conflicts. Unfortunately, this young man is presently in jail as a result of numerous arrests for domestic violence. The principle that he was unable to incorporate into his anger management strategy was never to use violence to resolve an emotional conflict. Sadly, we see this all too often while watching late night local news on television.

TOOL THREE TEST

1.   The three basic behavior styles of human beings are:

    A.   Submissive, Assertive and Explosive

    B.   Reserved, Amenable and Aggressive

    C.   Submissive, Assertive and Aggressive

    D.   Fat, Dumb and Happy

2.   Many have mismanaged strategies for dealing with their anger. We studied four wrong strategies. Which set is incorrect or wrong and not taught by ASN?

    A.   Concealer and Absorber

    B.   Pretender and Exploder

    C.   Over-Hander and Under-Attacker

    D.   Concealer and Exploder

3.   An angry person with an assertive behavior style tends to behave this way:

    A.   Concealer and Self-Absorber

    B.   Pretender and Exploder

    C.   Self-absorber and Pretender

    D.   All of the above

4.   Which one of the four mismanaged strategies appears to cause the most long term emotional and physical harm to the individual that has the anger problem?

    A.   Exploder

    B.   Pretender

    C.   Self-Absorber

    D.   Concealer

5.   To support an angry person's strategy, which of the five perverted methods is considered automatic and takes years of conditioning to appear totally peaceful?

    A.   Downsize

B.   Postpone or transfer

C.   Weaken or exclude it

D.   None of the above

6.   Of the five perverted methods that support an angry person's strategy, which method is used when one suddenly gets angry at someone else for no apparent reason?

A.   Downsize or postpone it

B.   Transfer it

C.   Weaken it

D.   Exclude it

7.   The anger log is an important tool in anger management. We connect each of the related dots in our personal anger log to get a true picture of our anger and our reactions to it.

A.   True

B.   False

8.   The critical point of tool three, the anger log, is that honest personal reflections must be observed from completing numerous anger logs of anger events.

A.   True

B.   False

9.   In tool three anger log materials, several recommended actions were encouraged. Which action was not recommended to you the student/client?

A.   Cultivate a new nature which is more peaceful and less angry

B.   Be angry in a good way, but not angry in a negative way

C.   Don't get over your anger, but keep it bottled up in your "backpack"

D.   Learn to accept the past, forgive the behavior, let go and move on with life

10. How many of the four mismanaged strategies and five perverted methods should a peaceful person be practicing in their relationship with loved ones and others?

A. All of the wrong strategies and all of the perverted methods

B. None of the wrong strategies and none of the perverted methods

C. Half of the wrong strategies and half of the perverted methods

D. All wrong strategies and none of the perverted methods

TOOL FOUR
RESPONSIBILITY MODEL

What is the number one cause of anger in America? It may surprise you to learn the number one cause of anger in America is lack of responsibility. In our society today, examples of this lack of responsibility are apparent everywhere. Parents are trying to rely on schools and churches to teach morals and values to their children, rather than exercise that responsibility themselves. The irresponsible and excessive use of drugs and alcohol is causing dysfunction in our families, and crime in our streets. Wherever you may live in the United States, tune in to your television for the local nightly news. In most areas the first half of that newscast amounts to the nightly crime report. Irresponsible driving is the force behind what we now term "road rage." This entire chapter could be filled with never-ending examples of irresponsibility and the anger it produces. The great need is to develop a sense of responsibility, where it has previously been lacking or non-existent.

The first component of developing a sense of responsibility is to turn to our higher power for help and guidance. Sometimes we tend to dismiss the thought that a higher power can be of sufficient help in our lives. Successful twelve-step programs recognize the benefit of a higher power. If irresponsibility is affecting our spiritual or temporal life, hopefully our higher power will help create in us a new responsibility model by which we can conduct our lives. A well-designed responsibility model includes brain wiring concepts, behavioral concepts, and personal rights, versus personal responsibility concepts. In addition, the critical areas of borders, conflicts, relationship types and responsibility priorities must be included. Ignoring one of these areas will result in a less than complete understanding of their vital role in reducing negative anger and increasing responsibility.

Brain Wiring Concept

The brain wiring concept includes three areas: mind, body and behavior. The anger-arousing perception of the mind is blaming our anger on others, playing the "blame game." An anger-reducing perception of the mind is accepting the fact that bad things happen sometimes. That is part of life. The central thought should be that life cycles with both good and bad things occurring for everyone at various times.

The second area of brain wiring is how our body reacts. Negative anger-intensifying habits are yelling, arguing, throwing objects and other negative actions. The anger-reducing perceptions of the body are relaxing, and having some fun. Do something you really enjoy and give your body a cooling off period.

The third area of brain wiring is our behavior. The anger-perverting behavior is to explode on others. However, exploding on others can provoke similar behavior on their part. The anger-controlling perception is using the **S-T-O-P** word concept, and assuming the role of peace keeper or peace maker.

To change the negatives to the positives, we must use the mind's power to change brain chemistry. With proper coaching and teaching, a person can:

- Develop a positive discipline
- Accept the past negatives of life
- Stop the blame game
- Forgive the person's behavior
- Strive to be more peaceful and less angry
-

To implement this brain wiring recovery plan, a person must:

- Re-define: Learn to call intrusive negative angry thoughts a brain malfunction
- Re-adjust: I must overcome this malfunction

- Re-concentrate: Focus on the positives, not the negatives

- Re-appraise: Focus daily on the above positive steps

Behavioral Concept (The Birdhouse)

Our minds are like a large birdhouse. Birds fly in and out of a birdhouse all day long, just as thoughts fly in and out of our minds, on a continuous basis. We cannot stop negative thoughts from entering our minds, but we certainly can keep them from "nesting" there. Negative anger can produce negative thought patterns. If we assign a bird species to four such thought patterns, we might have a blackbird, a hummingbird, a bluebird, and a vulture. We will look at the characteristic traits, the negative thinking, and the solution for the negative thinking for each of these species.

The first is the blackbird. The characteristics of this type of thinking are doom and gloom, and seeing only the worst in most situations. This thought pattern will produce extreme negativity, and no realization that at least 80% of the things we worry about never materialize. The  solution for this type of thinking is to think more realistically. Life does cycle for everyone. Reality dictates that we all will have some negative events in our lives, but we also will have many positive events. The ideal of realism is to focus on the positives and not the negatives.

The second is the hummingbird. The characteristics of this type of thinking are no advanced planning and a difficult time focusing. This thought pattern keeps a person from focusing on the important issues in life. The result of not focusing, can produce the familiar attitude: enjoy today and let tomorrow take care of itself. The solution for this type of thinking is to focus on the nuts and bolts of life. Another way to express this solution would be to focus and deal with the "gut issues" of your life. A hummingbird will dart from flower to flower without any real planning or focus. As humans we do not have that option. We must deal with the issues of our lives as they occur. Ignoring important issues will not prevent the next one from occurring, and thinking only about today will not stop tomorrow, nor will it help to prepare us for tomorrow.

The third is the bluebird. The main characteristic of this thinking is to be a loner who generally lacks self-esteem. This type of thinking does not allow for a necessary exchange of ideals. Characteristics of this type of individual are failure to fit in with others and difficulty relaxing in a group situation. This boils down to difficulty functioning in society. One solution of this thought pattern might be joining some enjoyable group, such as an adult education class or some civic organization. Also, this individual should try to develop at least one real friendship with a person he can respect and admire. This person could become not only a needed friend, but also could serve as a positive mentor.

The fourth bird is the vulture. The main characteristic of a vulture is never to give anyone a second chance, if he or she has caused hurt in your life. This type of person has probably been really hurt in the past and expects to be hurt in the future. This thought pattern will not allow for forgiveness of past harmful behaviors because of the expectation of these hurts recurring. The solution for these negative thoughts is to make a decision to forgive others, and to forgive oneself if necessary. Vultures also need to make a firm decision to stop dwelling on the past negatives in life.

In today's world we live in a difficult and demanding society.

However, in our thoughts we should try to concentrate on things that are true, honest, just and pure. In thinking these positive thoughts we can make permanent changes in our lives.

Personal Rights versus Personal Responsibility

In this important area of discussion, there is a popular misconception that love and responsibility are the same thing. In a perfect world they would be the same, but we do not live in a perfect world. An example is parents who love their children, but do not give them sufficient discipline, so that they have acceptable conduct. Another example would be those who state they love their spouse, but have intimate relationships outside their marriage. These are examples of using love to shield responsibility. Knowing that love and responsibility are not the same thing, we can make the following observations:

- Love should motivate responsibility
- Love should not shield responsibility
- Love is a continuing choice we make
- Love grows in a safe relationship (physical, emotional and spiritual)

Obviously there are different types and depths of love. *Eros* love is the sensual love a person has for a spouse or someone else. *Philo* love is the love we have for our close friends. *Storge* love is the love parents have toward their children. *Agape* love is the unconditional love our higher power has for each and every person.

Personal rights also include our responsibility toward ourselves. Self-anger results when we fail to exercise personal responsibility. Self-guilt will also arise from the lack of personal responsibility. In addition, anger toward a spouse will result from his or her perceived lack of personal responsibility.

Responsibility and Conflicts

To be human and alive means that we will have some

conflicts. Usually when the word *conflict* is used, we tend to think of a negative discussion or situation. In reality conflicts can be bad, but they may also be good and positive experiences. When bad conflicts occur, they can be disruptive in a relationship. In some cases they can completely destroy a relationship. One fact is certain: a serious struggle will require a great amount of energy to resolve that conflict.

Good conflicts can result in a number of positives. The first result is that they give us the opportunity to learn. We can determine how the other person really feels about the idea or situation under discussion. When we understand each other's position, we can grow closer in the relationship. The other good effect is to stop the stagnation if the two people have been avoiding the discussion because of opposite views.

Any discussion of conflicts always centers on what constitutes a real conflict. There are four areas that are at the heart of real conflict. These areas are opposing needs, opposing values, opposing goals or opposing interests. Real conflicts seem to have their root in one of these four vital areas. Our high divorce rate in the United States seems to indicate that the couples have not fully agreed upon these areas prior to or during marriage. Agreement and understanding are not options but necessities.

Responsibility and Borders

When people are asked if they have set good reasonable borders in their lives, there are a great variety of answers. These answers range from very good to absolutely terrible. Most people are somewhere in the middle of that wide range.

Borders are extremely important because they define who you are and what you are. You know yourself, but other people do not. Your borders give others a great insight into you as a person. Borders are the best way to keep the good in our lives, and to keep the bad out. Our borders should become our moral compass.

There are definite border laws that apply. The first law is that we must respect the borders of others. We desire to have others respect our borders, so we must show them the same courtesy. In evaluating others by their borders, we must understand we cannot change others. We may feel that they have borders that are unacceptable, but that is between them and their higher power.

The second law is that we are responsible to others, and at the same time we are responsible for ourselves. Trying to live a responsible life without borders is extremely difficult and for many, absolutely impossible. Therefore, good borders are critical components of our behavior. We are responsible for so many areas of our lives, including our emotions, attitudes, beliefs, values, desires, behavior and thoughts, just to name a few. We don't win every battle and sometimes we can step outside our borders, but we should keep trying to stay within them. Please note that you have an important option to agree to disagree, move on, and still be friends.

The best way to stay within your borders is to set your focus inside your borders, not outside them. Make your borders visible to others and make them changeable, if necessary, as the circumstances of your life occur. Do not be trapped in border myths that say you are being selfish or hurting others by setting borders. That is not valid reasoning. In reality you are simply setting good, reasonable borders so your life will be orderly and peaceful.

Relationship Types

Here is an interesting exercise for self-evaluation of your relationship with others, based on eight different personality traits. You know yourself better than anyone, so the ideal is to be completely honest with yourself. The personality traits on the left side are anger-reducing traits and those on the right side are anger-arousing traits. There is no pass or fail score, but you will see your strengths and your weaknesses. Score each trait with a number 1 to 5.

Review carefully each trait that you feel needs improvement. Remember, we all have areas of our lives that need improvement. The great football coaches always impressed on their players that winning every game, year after year, is not possible. However, they also impressed on these same players that not making the maximum effort to win, is unacceptable. We should maximize effort to improve in every area of our personality to reduce our anger level to an acceptable level.

RELATIONSHIP TYPES	
ANGER REDUCING (HEALTHY = 5 Points)	ANGER ROUSING (UNHEALTHY – 1 Point
HONEST HIGHER POWER	DISHONEST NO HIGHER POWER
OPENNESS ACCOUNTABLE	CLOSED UNACCOUNTABLE
TRUST AVAILABLE	DISTRUST UNAVAILABLE
DEDICATED UNSELFISH	NON-DEDICATED SELFISH

Responsibility Model

We have many areas of responsibility with which we must contend on a daily basis. These include the following:

- Country
- Family
- Higher Power
- Friends
- Work
- Extended Family
- Pets

Your challenge is to prioritize these areas in the order that you feel deserves the most responsibility. A typical priority list we see in our classes would be like the following:

- Higher Power
- Family
- Work
- Country
- Friends
- Extended Family
- Pets
- Hobbies

The question is who is missing from this list? The obvious answer is: you are missing. So where do you put yourself in this list? How responsible do you feel you must be to yourself? The answer is that you must be very high on the list. Ideally, you should place yourself under your higher power, and before family. The reason for this placement is that if you cannot be responsible to yourself, how can you expect to be responsible to your family, your work, your country, your friends, extended family and pets? Responsibility is like water; it runs downhill, not uphill. Assume responsibility for yourself first, and it will affect your other areas of responsibility, in a positive manner. Please note that we are not suggesting that you become self-centered, but higher power centered.

Another good exercise would be to prioritize your life today in the various areas of your relationship with your higher power, your family, your work, etc. Then determine what you would desire those relationships to be, if changes are needed. You will find that each positive change will probably demand a more responsible effort on your part to affect those changes.

Tool Four - Misguided Priorities Story

The negative effect of having a wrongly-prioritized list of

responsibilities can be devastating and lead to a life of imprisonment. Here is one such story: While teaching inmates the importance of prioritizing their areas of responsibility, one inmate in a class did the unthinkable. He broke down and started crying in front of the other 29 inmates in the classroom. In his life, he had put his family first and stolen from stores and burglarized homes to provide his parents, wife, and children whatever they desired. Because of this criminal lifestyle, he had spent 12 of the previous 14 years of his life incarcerated. This inmate broke down when he was finally able to see the importance of prioritizing his list by (1) putting his higher power first in his life, (2) putting himself second but not in a self-centered way and (3) putting his spouse and other family members closest to him third. It became obvious to him in class that his list of priorities was upside down. He had tried to take care of those he loved through criminal behavior and his badly-structured list resulted in years of incarceration.

Responsible Model Practice

"Prioritize Your Love Priority Today"

We know that we are very different individuals in most facets of our life. What is a priority to one individual may not be a high priority for another person. There is a good exercise to list your priorities as you see them in the circumstances of your life today. Please note below there is a current list of your priorities, which we invite you to complete, based on the categories that have been listed. Fill out the current list and then analyze it to see if those priorities are in the order you really desire. If they are not, complete the desired list and then take action to change your current priorities as much as possible.

Current List	Desired List

Our higher power should be able to help us see our core values and responsibilities more clearly. We should strive to become more responsible and make each day more pleasant and fulfilling.

TOOL FOUR TEST

1.   In tool four materials, we studied the Brain Wiring Concept. We learned that we can use our mind's power to change our brain chemistry.

    A.   True

    B.   False

2.   The Brain Wiring Recovery Plan has four important points. The points follow: Re-Define, Re-Adjust, Re-Concentrate and Re-Appraise.

    A.   True

    B.   False

3.   We studied four hypothetical angry birds in the Birdhouse Concept. The Blackbird characteristics were gloom and doom. The recommended solutions were to think really hard about the anger event, worry about it often and focus on being more negative.

    A.   True

    B.   False

4.   In the Birdhouse Concept, the Hummingbird thoughts are not to focus on issues and only enjoy today. The recommended solutions were to focus on the nuts and bolts of life which are the gut issues that are ongoing in your life.

    A.   True

    B.   False

5.   Under Personal Rights and Personal Responsibilities, several statements were shared about love and responsibilities. Which statement is not true?

    A.   Love grows in a safe relationship.

    B.   Love should not shield (hide) responsibility

    C.   Love and responsibility are the same

    D.   Love should motivate responsibility

6.   In the responsibility and conflicts area, we stated that all conflicts are bad and should be avoided if at all possible with our significant other or our spouse.

    A.   True

    B.   False

7.   In the responsibility and border and area, we made several points. Which following point is wrong?

    A.   Border lines help to reflect who I am and who I am not

    B.   Inside of my border lines, I am responsible for numerous things

    C.   Border lines should not be visible—they may offend someone

    D.   Border line laws apply-- we must be responsible for ourselves

8.   In Anger-Reducing relationship, we discussed at least eight qualities that couples should express toward each other-- which two are not Anger-Reducing qualities?

    A.   Honesty and Higher Power

    B.   Openness and Accountability

    C.   Trust and Availability

    D.   Non-Dedicated and Selfishness

9.   In the Responsible Model discussion, we recommended that people should prioritize their areas of responsibilities. Which two should be at the top of the list?

    A.   Spouse and children

    B.   Extended family and friends

    C.   Higher power and self

    D.   Hobbies and animals

10. Self-anger and self-guilt result from a lack of personal responsibility. The more responsible people become the less self-anger they tend to have in their lives.

    A.   True

    B.   False

TOOL FIVE
RECONCILIATION PROCESS

Reconciliation

Big word, but what does it mean? When you **reconcile with someone,** what does it mean to you?

_____

_____

_____

The blanks are for you to fill in what you think it means to reconcile with someone.

This is a definition that I consider to be reconciliation. Reconciliation could mean to bring back a friendship, to settle a quarrel, to harmonize a relationship, or to make a relationship right. As we begin the Reconciliation Process, I want us to look at several relationship or relational questions that we need to address. The first question is, "Where have we been?" In our past, we know the things that we have done right, and we know the things we have done wrong. We also know the victories and the defeats that we've had in our lives. The second question is, "Where are we now?" I want you to know right now how much I respect and admire you for the courage you have to come this far in the book. You are to be greatly admired and respected at this point in your life. The third question is, "Where are we going?" I sincerely believe there is a purpose and plan in the direction you're now moving in your life.

When two people are in a relationship the third question of "Where are we going?" must trigger another important question. That question is "Are we going to the same destination together?" Our high divorce rates many indicate men and women do not define their ultimate life goals as being the same. Those individuals who are not in a close relationship must also reconcile with themselves. The same questions would apply. The first question would be "Where have I been?" The second question would be "Where am I now?" The final question is "Where am I going?"

Whether people are in relationship or leading a single life, reconciliation is vitally important. Life can be so fast moving and complex that at times we forget the simple basics of asking ourselves about the past, the present and the future. Therefore, reconciliation is not a onetime event. Reconciliation is somewhat like the directions on a prescription bottle which reads "Take as needed."

To help in the reconciliation process, tool six will diagram a "High Way of Life." Look carefully at that highway and the various designation locations that are discussed. Everyone is on this emotional road somewhere at any given time. As you study this road you will see failures, disappointments, crisis points and a life of mediocrity. The goal will be to persevere and reach a "High Way" of life that brings peace, joy and contentment. Reconciliation is a necessary first step to start this "High Way" journey.

Now, I want to take a look at the Reconciliation Process with you. The Reconciliation Process has four parts to include the following:

- Accept the Past
- Forgive each Person's Behavior
- Let Go of Anger
- Move On With Life

Let's look at the first part together, which is **Accept the Past**. You may say to yourself, "I can't do that. You don't know all that I've been through in my life with these people you want me to forgive!" But I want you now to think about the reality for your life. There is nothing you can do about it. You can't go back and fix it. You can't go back and change it. The reality is that you can begin to accept the past hurts, because you are beginning to see there's absolutely nothing that you can do about it. How about that!

The second part is the hardest and always will be for you: to know that in your life, you have the courage and strength to **Forgive Each Person's Behavior** for all the ways they have hurt or wounded you. We are all human and when we have had a deep emotional hurt, we sometimes feel we will never be able to forgive. In fact, many people go through their entire lives without forgiving those who hurt them. The key point so many people do not consider is that forgiveness is not for the person we forgive. Forgiveness is for the person who offers the forgiveness, so that they can move on with their lives. Living a life of non-forgiveness, hate, bitterness and resentment is certainly a roadmap to an unhappy and unfulfilled life. We only pass through this life once, so why live that life with the negative feelings of non-forgiveness. Forgiveness now means "freedom now." It is vitally important to remember that it is the person's behavior that made you angry – not the person!

It may be well to remember that there are situations and incidents in our lives that will require our asking for forgiveness. It will become a necessary part of the process. An apology must include four important elements. The exclusion of any one of these elements could easily invalidate the apology. The four elements are as follows:

- Regret the action taken
- Understand the problem
- Accept your responsibility
- Be willing to do better

As I have stated, forgiveness takes strength and courage. In fact, for many it will be the most difficult human task they will ever experience. To help you accomplish this task, please seriously consider the following ten points of forgiveness. Each point is designed to create greater understanding of the forgiving process that will enable you to achieve the freedom giving act of forgiveness.

1. Healing past wounds is best done with a decision to forgive someone who wounded you; it is a specific action and more than feeling.
2. True forgiving occurs inside both our hearts and minds; what happens to the people we forgive depends on them.
3. Forgiving happens in stages: we rediscover the humanity of the person who wronged us, and we surrender our right to get even.
4. Higher power strength is required for us to forgive people fully for their behavior; we do not focus on who they are.
5. Forgiving is a beneficial journey; the deeper the wound, the longer the journey; it starts with an inner push to forgive others and **ourselves.**
6. Forgiveness is not about reunion with the person who broke our trust; there is no obligation to go back into a relationship as before.
7. We forgive others' behavior when we are ready to be healed, not just because it is the right thing to do.
8. Forgiving an unbelievable wrong does not make it acceptable, and it does not mean we intend to put up with it again.
9. We don't excuse the person's inappropriate behavior when we forgive them, and we do not surrender our rights to justice.
10. Real forgivers walk with their higher power and are not doormats, but willing mature humans who desire to be healed of their pain.

The third part is to **Let Go of Anger.** You may begin to realize that there is lots of hurt stuffed into your backpack you learned about in Tool 2. You've been hanging onto and carrying around for months or years but now in your own way, you can begin to let go. You know it's not doing you any good for you to keep hanging onto the hurt for _____ (the blank is for you to fill in now) months or years. Let's say that I have a backpack, and

I stuff a bunch of hurt, hatred, and bitterness toward someone into my backpack. After a period of time, you see me again and you ask," How long have you been carrying all of that stuff?" I say, "Oh, about two years now. I can't tell you how much I hate that person." Later on, I stuff more hurt, hatred, and bitterness toward the same person into my backpack. You ask me again, "How long have you been carrying all of that stuff now?" I say, "Oh, about five years now. But you know I want to be able to take this backpack off, slam it on the floor, and to be able to say that I want freedom!" I can now personally say to you, as you read this, my hope for you is that you too will know and have the freedom that you deserve. Therefore, the best way of letting go is to create an end of anger event and confess it to your higher power.

The fourth part is to **Move on With Life**. You don't know how the person or persons will receive your reconciliation with them. One thing you can honestly say to them at this time is, that "I don't know where our relationship will go from here, whether we will be together or apart. I want you to understand one thing, that with or without you, I am going to move on with my life. Do you understand?" Do you see the importance of being able now to move on with your life and have freedom? How the person responds to "Do you understand?" now places the responsibility on his shoulders. You have done what you honestly know to make the relationship right! In the reality for your life, you have done your part! You have been true to yourself, to the person or persons, and to a reconciliation process that is for real!

Now we are going to help you to use the reconciliation process to forgive the person or persons. There are some wonderful methods that we can identify to assist you in having your freedom. The following are significant methods, and only you will know if they are appropriate for you to begin to use:

- Face to Face with the Person
- Phone Conversation
- Writing a Letter or Card to the Person
- Individual "End of Anger Events"

Let's look at the first method together, which is **Face to Face with the Person**. If you're going to meet the person face-to-face, you are encouraged to do this in a public place. You may ask, why in a public place? The reason is that you want to be sure that there would be a safe and secure environment for the two of you to meet. In the event that the person would possibly begin to get out of control, then you have immediate help and witnesses to the person's negative behavior and action. What you will find is that the public place seems to cause the person to become more civil, and willing to hear what you are going to say, as you go through the reconciliation process. We prefer this method because it creates a vivid mental picture that you can recall later – it is the most desired method.

Let's look at the second method together, which is a **Phone Conversation**. An interesting perspective, that I know you will understand, can happen with the following real life scenario. You are speaking with the person and you begin to sense that they are beginning to lose control and not willing to hear you out. You have already planned what you are going to say in the reconciliation process, so you can make the decision to stop the call and know that you have done your part and can experience real freedom!

Let's look at the third method together, which is **Writing a Letter or Card to the Person**. As you write the letter or card, you are expressing your heart through each part of the reconciliation process. You want to be sure to have postal documentation to know that the letter or card was received. The person that receives your letter or card will have many opportunities to reread all that you have said to them. It is hoped that they will begin to see the sincerity and way that you are being real with them. Please understand that you may or may not ever receive a response from them. Remember, that you have done your part and can experience freedom.

Tool Five - Mother/Daughter Letter Story

I want to share a personal story with you about someone who carried the hurt in her life for 51 years toward her mother. As a little girl, teenager, young adult, and adult, she was verbally abused by her mother. She was never physically abused, but constantly felt that she was not ever doing things right to please her mother. She knew that she could not sit down and have a face to face conversation or share a telephone conversation with her mother, so she decided after 51 years to write her mother a letter. She wrote and told her mother how she was going to **Accept the Past**, how she was going to **Forgive Her Behavior**, how she was going to **Let Go of the Hurt** now, and finally, how she would **Move On with Her Life**, hopefully in a relationship with her mother. Her hope was for a mother/daughter relationship that would be wonderful after 51 years. Do you think that she ever received a response to the letter from her mother? Some at this time would say yes, some would say no. She was able to know that the letter was received, but she never received a response about the letter from her mother. The verbal abuse continued, but it didn't matter what her mother said, because she knew that she was free and had peace inside her own being.

The story continues that later in her mother's life, something began to change in the relationship. It could have been because of the letter's being read over and over by her mother. It could have been because of her mother's age. She never really knew, but she sensed a change in her mother, over time. There began a time where she heard her mother begin to speak of the value and the inner beauty of her own daughter. She heard a mature adult voice from her daughter expressing the love that her own daughter had for her as her mother. Yes, this beautiful lady did experience one thing when she put the letter in the mail. She can now honestly say with a strong voice and say out loud to the world . . . freedom.

Finally, let's look at the fourth method together, which is an **Individual End of Anger Event.** Let's say that you cannot do a Face to Face with the Person, Phone Conversation, or Write a

Letter or Card to the Person, then, I want to encourage you seriously to consider doing an Individual End of Anger Event.

The first **Individual End of Anger Event** is called **A Special Place**. I want you to begin to think of a special place that only you will remember where it will be located. As a suggestion, you may desire on a given day to go to the steps of a church, a special park, a place along a river or lake, or a special place that you will always remember where you were on that memorable day of your life. Now picture yourself at a special place and know already what you are going to say in the four parts of the reconciliation process. You are about to begin to do your own **Individual End of Anger Event.** Picture sitting there with the person you are going to forgive directly across from you. You share the four parts of the reconciliation process with them. You have done your part as you were led to do. You can now with a strong voice say out loud to the world . . . freedom! Let's say that six months have gone by and you can honestly remember the day and a special place that you had your own Individual End of Anger Event! Now, in your mind, let a year go by and you will be able to honestly remember again the day and a special place that you had your own Individual End of Anger Event. Five or more years could go by, and you could honestly remember that day and a special place where you forgave the person, had peace inside of your own being, and . . . freedom.

The second **Individual End of Anger Event** is called a **Coffee Can Burial**. I want to share a personal story with you of an individual named George who came to the Anger Solutions Network office with a need to reconcile with his ex-wife. He shared with one of the volunteer staff that he was going to remarry soon and did not want to bring his anger toward his ex-wife into his second marriage. He shared that he could not possibly do the Reconciliation Process with his ex-wife doing either a **Face to Face with the Person, Phone Conversation, or Write a Letter or Card to the Person**. He was asked to go home and bring back next week a list of all the things for which he was still angry with his ex-wife. He came back next week with a list that was three pages long. Our ASN volunteer realized that he was definitely angry with her and suggested that he go home and think of a special way he could use the reconciliation process in an **Individual End of Anger Event**.

He went home and this is how he began his **Individual End of Anger Event** for his life. On a Saturday morning while sitting at his breakfast room table, drinking coffee, and having a cigarette, an **Individual End of Anger Event** thought came to him. He got up from the table with his three pieces of paper, his cigarette lighter, empty coffee can, and then walked to the garage. There he got a shovel and headed to the back yard where he dug a hole and placed the coffee can in the hole. Next, he lit the three pieces of paper and held them over the coffee can until he could no longer hold the three pieces of paper. Then he dropped the remains of the papers into the coffee can in the hole. He watched the papers completely burn until the flame went out. Next, he got the shovel, placed dirt in the can, and placed the plastic lid back on the can. The remaining dirt was placed over the coffee can in the hole. Finally, George backed up about ten feet and, as he looked at the burial site, he stated how he was going to **Accept the Past**, **Forgive Her Behavior**, **Let Go of the Hurt**, and now be able to **Move On With His Life** without her.

The third **Individual End of Anger Event** is called a **Grave Site**. Bob came to the Anger Solutions Network office with a tremendous amount of anger in this life. He shared with Jay, the Anger Solutions Network Director, that he held this anger toward two of his friends that he killed who were raping his wife. Bob went to prison for twelve years, six months, and eighteen days. Since the double killing, Bob was able to reconcile with his higher power and himself, but not with the two men that he killed in Chicago. He needed help to let go of his anger toward those two guys that were his friends and partners in an illegal drug business. Jay suggested that Bob go to the cemetery in Chicago and use the reconciliation process as an **Individual End of Anger Event** with one of the men he had killed. Bob told Jay beforehand that he knew where one of the men was buried, but did not know where the second man was buried. A few weekends later, Bob flew to Chicago, met his mother, and they drove to the cemetery where the murdered man was buried. Once at the large cemetery, he realized that the cemetery office was closed on Saturday, and he could not locate the grave site. He then observed a man cutting the grass with a tractor lawn mower. Bob decided to stop the grass cutter and asked if he knew how he could locate a certain grave site. The worker asked Bob which grave site he wanted to visit. Bob said, "I am looking for Joe Lopez's grave." To Bob's amazement, the workman said, "I know exactly where that grave is located, and I will walk you to it." Upon arriving at the exact grave site, Bob asked, "How did you know within this large cemetery exactly where this one grave was located?" To the shock of Bob, the workman said, "I visit this grave every day because he is my son." The workman noticed the shock expressed on Bob's face and asked this question, "Who are you and why are you here this weekend?" Bob then told the father that he had flown from San Antonio, Texas, to forgive his son, Joe, for an act that had been committed toward his wife. Since the father did not know how his son had died, Bob provided all the details and then asked the father to also forgive him for his actions against his son. These two men later hugged, cried, and reconciled with each other, and then the father departed for work and left Bob to speak privately with Joe at the grave site Bob went through the entire reconciliation process, just as Jay had suggested to him, and just as if Joe was alive and could speak to him.

Once back at the car where his mother was waiting for him, Bob stopped to call Jay on the cell phone. Bob told Jay, while crying like a baby, this was one of the happiest day of his life. He also said that he felt, "light as a feather, now that the anger was gone from his backpack and from his life." Bob was able to have peace inside of his own being and . . . freedom.

I now want you to think about this **Individual End of Anger Event** at the **Grave Site** with the following questions:

- What are the chances that Bob could locate the grave site on his own?

- What are the chances that Bob would be at the cemetery on a day that the father of Joe was close by cutting the grass?

Yes, there is a plan for our lives and by being open to that plan we can experience freedom.

To continue the story, Bob came home but did not ever find out where the other man was buried. On a given day and in his own **Special Place** as if he was at the **Grave Site**, he was able to go through the entire reconciliation process again and forgive the other man. Again, Bob was able to have true peace inside of his own being and . . . freedom!

Reconciliation Process – Face to Face with the Person. . . A Personal Story

We can illustrate the reconciliation process with a real life situation between a son named Ben and his dad. Ben felt a genuine need and desire to reconcile with his dad. He asked his dad to meet him in a public place and his dad agreed to meet. Ben now had the opportunity to speak to his dad from the heart.

To begin the conversation, Ben relates to his dad his feelings of hurt when his dad showed virtually no interest in his activities in his youth. Whether it was in junior high or high school sport or a drama play, the dad did not attend to see Ben perform. While these absences were disturbing, Ben has even a deeper hurt and resentment. He tells his dad he cannot remember even one time receiving a hug or having his dad tell Ben that he loved him. Ben tells his dad of his honest and sincere desire to forgive him. He also tells his dad he has accepted the past and is letting go of the hurt and resentment and is moving on with his life. Ben finishes his comments by asking his dad this important question "Do you understand?"

At this point, the important fact is that Ben has started the reconciliation process. His dad could respond negatively by ignoring Ben's comments and refusing to take any responsibility for his past behavior. The ideal outcome would be for the dad to respond positively by admitting his past mistakes, tell Ben that he does love him and desires a closer relationship in the future.

A third alternative would be for both Ben and his dad to agree to meet again so that they both would have sufficient time to reflect on the past and their future relationship. Perhaps at this next meeting they could both admit shortcomings and failures. There are always two sides to one degree or another in any relationship. The ideal ending would be that both Ben and his dad would become fully engaged in the reconciliation process. Hopefully, they could look each other in the eye and genuinely both state "I love you."

The outcome of this story is positive rather than negative. If the dad had not reacted in a positive manner, Ben would still have had the self-satisfaction of reconciliation. He had **accepted** the past, **forgiven** his dad's behavior, **let go** of the anger and **moved on** with his life. Ben can now say with confidence, "close the curtain, the game is over."

Tool Five - Give up the Idea Story

I was teaching a small group of people who were training to become certified facilitators for Anger Solutions Network. One of the participants had been in prison twice and had deep feelings, that because of his past, he would always have guilt, shame and self-blame. He very seldom attended chapel on Sunday, but one particular Sunday he felt the desire to attend.

That Sunday a guest chaplain visited the prison and held the regular worship service. My student said that the chaplain made one comment that struck the right chord in his heart and mind that changed his life. The chaplain's statement was "**Give up on the idea of having a better past.**" For the first time he actually understood the past is the past. The past is history and cannot be relived nor can it be changed. That morning he put his past behind him and looked only to a meaningful and productive life ahead.

TOOL FIVE TEST

1.   The Reconciliation process starts with some basic questions. What are they?

   A.   Where have I traveled, where did I live and where do I want to move next?

   B.   Where was my spouse, where is my spouse now and where they are going next?

   C.   Where have I been, where am I now, and where am I going in the future?

   D.   Who is the President, who is the Governor, and who is the Mayor?

2.   How many parts are there to the reconciliation process?

   A.   Two parts

   B.   Three parts

   C.   Four parts

   D.   Five parts

3.   In the reconciliation process, I must forgive the person's

   A.   Culture

   B.   Negative behavior

   C.   Race

   D.   General behavior style

4.   In the reconciliation process, it is best to do the following first step:

   A.   Accept the broken past

   B.   Try to tell yourself it never happened

   C.   Blame your anger on the person's parents or friends

   D.   Blame you anger on yourself or your higher power

5.   Forgiveness in the reconciliation process is critical. One correct point follows:

   A.   Forgiveness is a specific act and more than a warm feeling

   B.   Forgiveness never happens in stages; we just hurry up

and do it right now

C.   We don't need a higher power to forgive someone's behavior fully

D.   Forgiveness is about a reunion with the one that broke our trust

6.   In the reconciliation process, forgiveness is critical. One of main point follows:

A.   Forgiving an intolerable wrong makes it tolerable to bear it again and again

B.   Forgiving means we intend to keep putting up with the wrong forever

C.   We excuse the person's wrong behavior for his or her personal benefit

D.   Real forgivers walk with their higher power and are not doormats

7.   If possible, the most desired method to reconcile with someone is to do the following:

A.   Send an email to them and copies to the other known parties

B.   Write and mail a hand-written detailed letter with all the facts

C.   Meet with them eyeball to eyeball in a public place

D.   Call the person on the phone, cry a lot and get it over as soon as possible

8.   Prior to forgiving, one should apologize to the person. The elements of apology are:

A.   Regret the action, understand the problem, accept the responsibility and be willing to do better

B.   Regard the action, question the problem, pass the responsibility to someone else and tell them you may or may not do better

C.   Forget the action, discount the problem, remove responsibility and don't say a word about the event to anyone

D.   Regret the action, misunderstand the problem, don't accept the responsibility and be willing to do worse

9.   Many have problems really letting go of anger. Actions that may help follow:

A.   Recreate the event with the person, friends and with others

B.   Create an End of Anger Event and confess your anger to your higher power

C.   Make the other angry person confess and change his or her vantage point

D.   Try to forget the event, blame others for the anger and not yourself

10.   Our critical point about real reconciliation is listed below at A, B, C or D.

A.   Real reconciliation is somewhat recommended to moving forward peacefully with your personal life

B.   Real reconciliation may or may not be suggested to moving forward peacefully with your personal life

C.   Real reconciliation is central to moving forward peacefully with your personal life

D.   Real reconciliation is not required to moving forward peacefully with your personal life

TOOL SIX
THE HIGH WAY JOURNEY

Life is a journey and we all travel on life's emotional high way. In this final chapter, we will examine destination points on this high way and the difficulties we may encounter on our journey. First we need to look at the emotional roadmap of the high way before we start the journey. The emotional roadmap and the various destinations can be illustrated with the following classroom graphic, which also reflects possible characteristics for each emotional roadway of life.

Low Road / High Way Realities

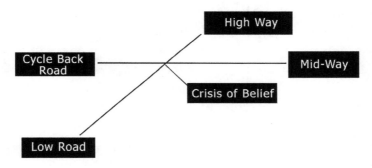

The journey of life does not begin at the same starting point for everyone. There are individuals that are born into loving families and their behavior will exhibit happiness, joy, and a deep sense of spiritual values. Others are born into dysfunctional families, and their learned behavior is clouded by trauma, rejection and anger. To study and understand the high way journey concept, we will follow the journey of the person born in dysfunctional circumstances. As this person matures and experiences all the negative emotions surrounding his life, he may very easily find himself in an anger hole. A discussion of the anger hole seems to be in order.

There are three ways people can find themselves in an anger hole.

- Thrown in
- Slipped in
- Jumped in

The depth of the anger hole can range from unrighteous anger, to the bottom of the pit, which is rage. An individual can find himself in the anger hole through no fault of his own. For example, parents might receive a phone call from the police stating that their son or daughter was arrested for selling drugs. The parents are now in the anger hole. They had no idea their child was involved with drugs in any way, shape or form. They did not slip in or jump in; they were thrown in by these unwanted circumstances.

Most people will slip into the anger hole. It will not be one big incident but smaller circumstances or incidents that cause a slow but steady decline into the hole over a period of time. At some point people will realize they are in an anger hole and will start to reflect on what went wrong to bring them to this undesirable position. They slipped into the hole one small step at a time. One small argument, one comment, or one reaction, but all add up to the constant slippage.

Unfortunately, some people simply jump in the anger hole through their own actions. This usually occurs because we try to control others by giving them unsolicited advice. When they reject our advice we may be angry, but it is really self-inflicted anger at that point. Another way to jump into the anger hole is to become angry when your borders are not respected, while others are expecting you to respect their borders. Again, this is a self-inflicted one-way ticket to the anger hole.

In discussing people born into an angry, dysfunctional home, we can agree they were thrown into the anger hole as a result of their angry learned behavior. As such people mature, there may certainly be a desire to move out of the anger hole and start up the highway to a better life. There will be two ways out of the anger hole:

76

- People can help – temporarily
- Higher power can help –permanently

Hopefully, as this person starts the maturing process, someone will become a non-angry role model. This could be a friend, a teacher or any other person that could have a positive influence. The real hope is that someone will introduce the concept of a higher power to this individual. Such an introduction would be a permanent help on a life-long basis. This person can now start moving out of the anger hole, and begin the journey away from the low road of life that has negative characteristics such as negative anger, poor attitude, guilt, shame, non-forgiveness.

As we follow a person coming out of the anger hole, let's give him a name and call him John. He has been in the anger hole for as long as he remembers, but he does have the desire to change. Life has not been easy for John. He was reared in a very dysfunctional home. His father was an alcoholic and had a difficult time staying employed and supporting his family. His mother seemed always to have an angry attitude. She was forced to work to help support the family in addition to all the other pressures of raising a family. John is one of three children and both his brother and his sister are subjected to the same type of negative feelings, negative pressures and negative emotions that would be present in this type of home atmosphere. We can truly state John is on the emotional low road of life. The characteristics and attitudes of low road living are seen on the following graphic:

Low Road

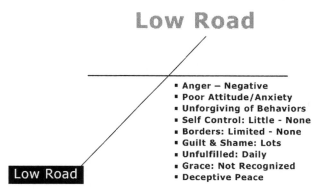

- Anger – Negative
- Poor Attitude/Anxiety
- Unforgiving of Behaviors
- Self Control: Little - None
- Borders: Limited - None
- Guilt & Shame: Lots
- Unfulfilled: Daily
- Grace: Not Recognized
- Deceptive Peace

Low Road

At first, things go fairly easily. John has used drugs in the past and has overused alcohol. He makes some firm promises to himself to quit these habits or at least cut down on their use. As the days and weeks go by, John is starting to feel more positive about himself. Then one day John notices he really has the strong feeling that he needs a few drinks, and perhaps his desire for drugs also returns. John has just reached the crisis point of belief.

Crisis of Belief

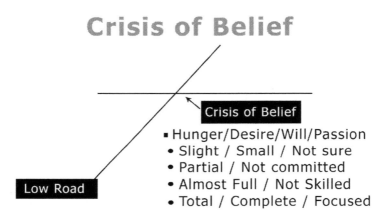

- Hunger/Desire/Will/Passion
- Slight / Small / Not sure
- Partial / Not committed
- Almost Full / Not Skilled
- Total / Complete / Focused

John is not the only person to go through a crisis point. Most people have a few crisis points in their lives. There are endless reasons for a crisis. A few would be health issues, addictions, financial problems and failed relationships. The question is not whether we will have a crisis in our life, but rather can we work through the crisis. The answer to that question will be how much hunger/desire/will/passion do we have to work through the difficult times. Will the effort be slight, partial, almost full or will it be a total and complete effort? John will have to make a total and complete effort to work through this crisis point. Anything less will almost assuredly fail. If failure does occur, John will move to the cycle back road and the process will have to begin again.

Cycle Back Road

- Looking Back - Looking Forward
- No Forgiveness - Forgiving
- No Reconciliation - Reconcile
- Deceptive Peace - Dark Peace

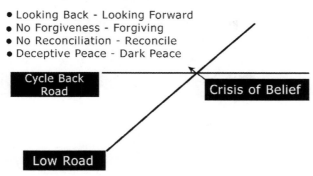

If a person constantly lives on the low road and is unable to work through the crisis points, at some point he will risk permanent failure. Eventually, anyone in this situation will become physically, mentally and spiritually exhausted. The cycle back road is paved with few feelings of forgiveness, little reconciliation, and feelings of hopelessness. At this crucial point, John must turn his mind to his higher power, to help him understand the physical and mental pressures that will accompany his return to the low road.

When we feel our challenges are overwhelming, and beyond our ability to solve a problem or work through a crisis, we need to remember that many other people have been successful in overcoming the crisis, they faced. They accomplished this with a total and complete desire to succeed with the help of their higher power.

John now tries again and once more he hits the crisis point. This time he makes the maximum effort and with the help of his higher power, he is successful in working through the crisis. He does experience some positive changes in his life and travels the road to the midway point. John notices that his anger has become more neutral, his attitude is better, and he sets a few borders. This is a critical phase in John's life because he is starting to feel some peace. This peace is what we could still recognize as a dark peace. The reason we can classify it as a dark peace is that it is certainly better than the low road, but the problem is that the mid-way does not bring true happiness and a secure a real peace of mind. The midway is the place that most people in our society live today. They are not really unhappy, but not living a full and abundant life. There is also the danger of drifting back to retest a crisis point.

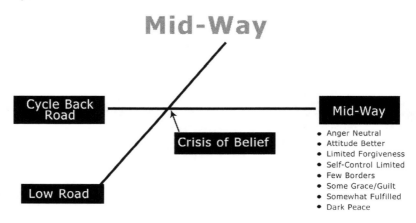

Slowly, John starts feeling the need to elevate his life and fill an emptiness he has always experienced. This feeling could be expressed as a true "crisis of belief" because it will require a decision that involves a lifetime commitment. John then makes the most important decision of his life. That decision is that with the help of his higher power he will completely change his feelings of defeat into feelings of accomplishment, and overcome the negative past. He is no longer in a crisis mode. The uncertainty and insecurities of his life transform into feelings of peace and fulfillment. His emotions become positive rather than negative in a variety of areas. Over the next weeks and months his attitude is much improved. From a spiritual perspective, he becomes more compassionate, and has a sense of self-control that will allow him to set reasonable border lines in his life. At this point he has certainly arrived on the high road.

High Way

All of us are on a journey in our lives. Reaching the high road is more difficult for some than for others. It depends to a great extent on an individual's motivation and ability. Some people are highly motivated, but lack ability and skills. Others have a high degree of ability and skills, but lack motivation. The tools outlined in this book are the basis for a change guide or plan for the negative anger emotion. The keys to success will be the use of the tools, to the best of your ability, starting to use the tools immediately. Change will only occur with implementation. The best implementation plan is to make a personal covenant with yourself and your higher power. Use the covenant outlined after the following three stories as a guide. Actually write it out, sign and date it and then start using the tools today.

Tool Six - Furniture Story

The effects of negative anger can be devastating and sometimes just simply beyond belief. Here is one such true story that would qualify:

We worked with a relatively young couple who were on the verge of a divorce. They were extremely secure financially and had two beautiful young daughters. From all appearances this young couple had achieved the American Dream, and had every reason to look at the future with confidence and optimism. It seemed they had achieved what most people in their age group would consider a high degree of success. Unfortunately, they were unable to reconcile and a divorce did occur.

An anger issue which developed in their marriage was the cause of the divorce. This anger issue, believe it or not, was over a piece of furniture. This piece of furniture was one that they were having made to order at a furniture factory on the east coast. The husband was unaware of some style changes and fabric changes the wife had made after the initial order. These changes were made over a period of time and resulted in a significant increase in the cost. When the item was finally delivered and the husband became aware of the final cost, he became extremely angry. As happens in so many cases, words were exchanged by both parties that were hurtful and difficult to retract.

It is hard to believe that a piece of furniture could be the basis of a divorce. This couple reached a crisis point in their lives, as pointed out in our sixth tool. The problem was that they did not have the total and complete desire to work through that crisis point, and they and their children will suffer the emotional consequences.

Tool Six - Shattered Door Story

During my drinking days, I had quite a temper. Though I would not admit to it, I would fly off the handle at the slightest thing. I quit drinking and things became better; however, there were times when the old behavior would return.

My family and I lived in a house where we did not have the key to the front door. Therefore, I had instructed the family that they were to ensure the chain was off the door whenever we left home or, someone had the key to the back door. I was fairly confident no one would attempt to break into the house from the front since it was close to the street and on a military installation.

We left for church one Sunday morning and one of the kids pocketed the key to rear door. Upon returning home he forgot he had the key, and the back door was locked. I went around to check the front door, only to find the chain was on. I had an instant flare up. I didn't stop to think. I put my shoulder into the door with all I had. I am not a big man. At the time I weighed about 155 pounds but it was enough to shatter the door frame and take the door off the hinges. As I stepped through the door, my son and the rest of the family were coming through the house. That did not help. I was ready to get a piece of him until my wife stepped in and asked how we were going to secure the house for the night. It gave me enough time to simmer down a bit.

I apologized to my wife and the kids for my poor behavior and, of course, reminded them about the rules for putting on or taking off the door chain. My wife had a friend who worked in Civil Engineering and the friend was able to get one of her co-workers to come out that day and fix the door. That was the day that I learned how important it was to **S-T-O-P**, and take the High Way, rather than cycling back.

Tool Six - Mid-Way Bipolar Story

Sometimes clients are unable to find real, lasting peace in their life from our program, and they continue to live on the midway road of life. One reason is that outside medical assistance is needed. One such story illustrates this point. Jim completed our program, but it seemed not to have the desired result in his life. Neither Jim nor I could understand why. We both concluded that perhaps he had not focused on the material or completed the specific assignments, as directed. Therefore, we made the decision to repeat the course. As we approached the end of the second series of six one-on-one sessions, I sensed we were only making limited progress. I talked to Jim's wife about his lack of progress and learned she believed he was bipolar. However, he had never been evaluated for this disorder. Collectively, we came to a decision to have Jim medically evaluated. The doctor to whom we referred Jim did conclude that he was bipolar and prescribed the appropriate medication to give him the assistance he needed. This medication, along with his anger management tools, helped Jim to control his emotional highs and lows. Today he is considered one of our poster children in a program which was supplemented with the appropriate medication.

MY PERSONAL COVENANT WITH MY HIGHER POWER AND MYSELF

Realizing now that I have the power
to control my anger,
I will honestly attempt to use
the tools and my anger plan
to the best of my ability.

Signed _____

Date _____

TOOL SIX TEST

1. In our tool six discussions, there are three ways to get into our anger hole(s).

    A. Thrown in by learned negative behavior, slipped in and jumped in

    B. Thrown in, slipped in with negative friends and jumped in

    C. Thrown in, slipped in and jumped in because of my wrong desires

    D. All the above

2. In our tool six graphic of the roadways of life, there are four roads. They are:

    A. High way road, Mid-way road, Cycle back road and Low road

    B. Hacker way road, Back-slider road, Coward-back road and Lower road

    C. High hand road, Milky-way road, Return back road and Loner road

    D. High way road, Mid-way road, Come-back road and Devil road

3. People living on these four emotional roads of life have certain characteristics. People living on the Low Road tend to reflect these characteristics:

    A. Reflect negative anger, many boundaries and divine peace.

    B. Reflect poor attitudes, lots of guilt and are compassionate givers.

    C. Reflect unforgiveness, self-centered and are most confident with peace.

    D. Reflect little self-control, little to no boundaries and are takers in life.

4. At the Crisis of Belief intersection, one must choose one of

four road directions.

    A.   Slight hunger, desire, will or passion probability will choose Any Way

    B.   Total hunger, desire, will or passion probability will choose High Way

    C.   Almost total desire, will or passion probability will choose Loud Way

    D.   Partial hunger, desire, will or passion probability will choose No Way

5.   People living on these roads have certain characteristics. Cycle Back type people:

    A.   Cycle from looking forward to looking even further into the future

    B.   Cycle from reconciling with big people to reconciling with little people

    C.   Cycle from forgiving big personal items to forgiving little personal items

    D.   Cycle from deceptive peace to dark peace and back to deceptive peace

6.   Equipped with six new anger management tools, new insights, and new concepts, graduates must now provide the _____ to have real change in their lives.

    A.   Guts or intestinal fortitude

    B.   Help from other angry friends

    C.   Personal willpower

    D.   Additional training from a counselor

7.   To experience real anger change, one must possess these two personal items:

    A.   Character and friends

    B.   Real wants and overcome limitations

    C.   Head knowledge and street smarts

D.   Education and a good job

8.   You were encouraged to read and sign an anger management commitment.

    A.   This personal commitment is not important at all

    B.   This personal commitment may or may not be important

    C.   This personal commitment is not worth signing

    D.   This personal commitment is critically important to you

9.   This is the critical point of tool six High Way change plan.

    A.   High Way living is possible only with an implemented change plan

    B.   High Way living may be possible with any conceived change plan

    C.   High Way living can't be possible with an implemented change plan

    D.   High Way living is not at all possible with any such change plan

10.   Six anger management tools were shared in this course. Which answer is correct?

    A.   Tools one to three are the most important anger management tools

    B.   Tools four to six are the most important anger management tools

    C.   Tools one through six are all important tools in my tool bag for life

    D.   Tools are just tools for someone else to use when they need them

SUMMARY

There is an old saying that we are all like snowflakes, because there are no two exactly alike. That saying certainly has validity when we describe how we use or misuse our emotions, especially the emotion of negative anger. The purpose of this book is to create a flow of logical thinking in the area of managing negative anger. In presenting the six anger management tools, our goal is to create concepts and precepts to accomplish that purpose.

The order in which the tools are presented has a definite reasoning. Over the years of our experience with thousands of clients, the order of the tools was dictated by which subjects were the most critical and required immediate attention.

The first tool is the **S-T-O-P** word, and the second tool is the **Confident Persuasive Message.** These two tools are generic in nature and should be used by each and every person when confronted with an angry situation. The last four tools, **Anger Log, Responsible Model, Reconciliation Process and High Way Journey,** are more personal in nature. They require each individual to do an honest evaluation of his anger emotion, which includes the way a person acts and reacts under the influence of anger. It also includes what individuals feel are their responsibility priorities. Once these areas are addressed, many people realize that reconciliation and forgiveness play a vital role in moving forward with a life without negative anger. The final step is an honest and in-depth realization of where we are on our emotional road of life. This includes working through some difficult crisis points, which most people experience to one degree or another.

One of the most exciting aspects of our ministry is the fact that we never know what anger management tool will be most significant to any particular individual. We are sometimes surprised and happy when we hear someone state, "That's what I needed to hear," or "I never thought of it in that way, and it really makes sense to me."

We have worked with over 35,000 people, and that figure increases every year. With rare exception, these are good people who are just having an anger problem. Some of these problems are temporary in nature and some last for longer periods. In any event, we have certainly learned not to judge people based on one single emotion. We all have both strength and weakness. We do not have to fight our battles alone. Help is available through good anger management programs, and turning to our higher power for guidance and direction.

OPTIONAL ACTIVITIES

Tool One S-T-O-P Word Optional Activities

We have learned the **S-T-O-P** word in an acronym reference to enable us to remember it as needed in our daily lives. I want to share a time when I was angry and did not handle my anger very well. If I had known the S-T-O-P word at that time, I would have saved an unnecessary exchange of words with the other person and undue stress to myself.

I went through excessive training with my dachshund to be able to take her to Brooke Army Medical Center (BAMC) to visit patients, including the soldiers there recuperating from injuries while serving our country. Once a year, we had to return for a test with our dog for the instructor to observe whether or not commands were still obeyed. There were about 16 other people present to participate with their dogs also. It soon became my turn. The first thing I had to do was put my dog on a "sit and stay" command. I then walked away from her, and it was her job to remain seated for 30 seconds and then come to me when I called her. She did great on that. The next very important command while visiting in a hospital setting, is to "leave it." The purpose of that is so the dog will not eat a pill or anything dangerous on the floor. I then took her and put her on a stay again, but this time when I called her, she had to come to me and not pick up any bones on the floor, which were to represent pills. I called her and she varied from the path to me for a second, going toward a bone, and I said, "leave it." She did not pick it up, but from where the instructor was standing, she thought she did. She reprimanded me and told me I did not give her a command. I knew my dog did not pick up the bone, so I very aggressively said to the instructor, "She did not pick up the bone and I did give her a command." We argued back and forth, and I got emotional over defending my dog because she was absolutely defenseless in this setting. I just felt like both of us were being reprimanded for something she did not do, and for something I did do but, was not believed. The instructor allowed my dog to stay in the program because she knew how much she was loved by the patients at

BAMC. I felt relieved about that, but I felt bad about the damage done to the relationship between the instructor and me. Now that I have learned the S-T-O-P word, I would have handled that situation differently. The first thing, when trying to defend my dog, I would have thought about the **S** in **S-T-O-P** and kept my mouth shut. The letter **T** would be next, so I would have self-evaluated the way I was **THINKING** at the time. I would remember that I am an adult and not a child, which is probably where my defense was at the time. The next letter being the **O** for **OPEN** would have reminded me I certainly needed to process the fact that the instructor was probably standing in a place that made it difficult to see what happened. Lastly, remembering the **P**, I would recognize I was having a **PROBLEM** with anger and remind myself I need to get control quickly.

Now it is your turn to participate. Think of a time when you became angry and exchanged words. You might want to write this down. Then go back, walk your way through the story again and how you would handle the situation differently if you had, at the time, known the stop word tool. This tool often helps me diffuse my anger and keep it under control. Then I become the winner in the situation.

Tool One S-T-O-P Word
Brain Chemistry

I like to get my students involved with hands-on materials to have a better understanding of the information being learned. In addition, I want them to have fun while making application of the chemicals. The correct term for this is a **manipulative.**

First of all, we go over all the chemicals that are held in the chemical sac, what they mean, and what role they play in the body when triggered.

After detailed discussion of each chemical, I then pass out cards to the students with a chemical word written on each one. Sometimes I give one card to each participant. At other times, I put them in groups to discuss the correct response, and one person will hold up the group choice after discussion among themselves. I always encourage the students to help each other draw a conclusion about the correct answer, before holding up the card. The next step is for me, the instructor, to read about 10 scenarios that will be the result of a particular chemical or chemicals being charged and released. For example, if I say to the students, "that chocolate candy is so good!" The correct card to hold up would be ... **Endorphin**. Most of us receive pleasure from a great piece of chocolate candy or cake! I think it is also beneficial to ask the students to share with me the reason for the choice they made. This helps me know there is understanding of the chemical and not just a choice. When we are finished with the game, the students do have a better understanding of the chemicals and the role they play when released.

List of the Chemicals that are released according to the occasion:

Chemical:	Function:
1. Adrenaline	Energy, Alertness
2. Endorphin	Pleasure, Enjoyment
3. Serotonin	Peaceful, REM sleep
4. Dopamine	Reward, Euphoria
5. Norepinephrine	Anger, Righteous Anger
	Anger, Unrighteous Anger, Wrath, Fury,
	Rage

Now it is your turn to play the game, remembering sometimes there can be more than one chemical released for the occasion. If you have someone to interact with at this time, I would encourage you to do so, for discussion is helpful. Then get paper and pencil to number 1-10. Write beside each number the chemical you believe fits the scenario. There might be more than one chemical for each answer, depending on your view. The answers are on the next page for you to check. I only wrote one chemical answer for each, but you might see it differently. The

most important thing to remember is, do the answers make sense according to the definitions?
1. My little girl is running across the street and a car is coming!
2. I feel so peaceful and rested.
3. If my boss does that to me one more time, I'm going to quit!
4. I have been in Iraq for two years and today I am going home!
5. My husband is having a heart attack. Please send an ambulance to this address quickly!
6. I thought she was my friend, but she continues to tell lies about me. I feel like beating her up!
7. If a dog is attacking a child and you want to help, which chemical would be released?
8. I will get to see my baby for the first time today!
9. I so enjoy spending time with you, my friend.
10. When I lay my head on my pillow at night, I feel at peace.

Answers to the Chemical Scenarios:
1. Adrenaline
2. Serotonin
3. Norepinephrine
4. Dopamine
5. Endorphin
6. Norepinephrine
7. Adrenaline
8. Dopamine
9. Endorphin
10. Serotonin

I believe it is important for us to learn these chemicals and what happens to us when they are released. As we analyze these, we have a better understanding of why we react the way we do at times. In dealing with norepinephrine, we must stop it, for trying to control a chemical that is released at 280 miles per hour, is a difficult train to stop! It is imperative for you and me to use the Stop Word Tool. That might be a life saver someday for us! You will feel blessed as you move forward with your life.

Tool One S-T-O-P Word
Body on the Floor

The purpose of this manipulative activity is to give a very powerful visual of what anger does to our bodies, sometimes without us realizing the impact, until many years later.

Some of the physical responses to anger include the following: dilation of pupils, increase of blood surges, elevation of blood pressure, increase in breathing rate, increase of adrenaline, and tightening of muscles. These responses can, and will have an effect on your body.

The next thing we do is ask a volunteer to lie on the floor and another volunteer to trace around that person with chalk. When this is completed, each class member receives a card with a physical response on it. Because we have muscles all over our bodies and they need to be recognized in this response, I have at least six cards available with "tightening of muscles." Then each class participant will receive a card with a physical response written on it to place on the body in the appropriate place. When this activity is completed, there is an awakening visual of what anger does to our body.

As an online program, I suggest writing these responses on masking tape and placing them on a drawing of a person. When I saw this body covered with all the physical responses, I realized for the first time how all my anger has affected my body. At my age, I should not be having so many health issues. Please allow these tools you are learning to help you get rid of your anger. This is not easy and it certainly will take a high degree of work on your part.

Tool One S-T-O-P Word
Cycle of Addiction

I have learned that if I have any kind of addiction, there will be a cycle involved. Examples of addictions are: drugs, alcohol, food, etc.

The order of an addiction cycle is ... Strong Feelings, Remembered Pleasures, Telling Self Lies and Believing Them, Use, Binge, Crisis, Emerge Remorseful, Solemn Resolves, Seek Help, and finally Recovery.

I think it is extremely important to evaluate my life and face my own addiction. As I think about this, I go through each part of the cycle, relating it to my own life, thus making application and understanding of how it works for me. For example, when I look at Strong Feelings, what is pulling me to my addiction? If this is acted upon, I will then go to the Remembered Pleasures and then possibly the cycle will continue. I know it is possible to break this cycle, and I **can** do this!

I believe remembering the order of the cycle is very important. At any time, I can think to myself...what is coming next? Hopefully this will help break the cycle before it is out of control.

When teaching a class, I pass out cards with a part of the cycle written on each one. I ask a group of students to go up and put the words, around the circle, in the correct order as the cycle occurs. I do encourage the students to help each other if needed. I have asked the students the purpose of this activity and they tell me, "I need to know what is coming next and hopefully stop it from occurring."

For those taking the class online, I would suggest you draw a circle and, without looking at the answers, write the words that are included in the addiction cycle. If need be, do it again until it is correct.

I also believe it is important for everyone to know enough about this cycle to know where to break it. For me, I believe it must be after Recovery and that first tinge of Strong Feelings. That is where all my determination to change my life has to be as strong as steel. I believe the concept of higher power help is vitally important in addiction recovery. This has been a very important part of the extremely successful twelve-step programs.

As the writer of these manipulative ideas and the role-playing examples, I have had to deal with many things I have written about. Perhaps that is the reason I have been called to teach anger management in the ladies detention center and other places where I have found an open door. It is my joy to help and encourage others to maximize their potential with the help of their higher power. At Anger Solutions Network we believe that everyone has the potential to help others make a positive contribution through service to others. No one is left out and everyone should be included in reaching their potential.

Tool Two
Confident Persuasive Message Optional Activities
Cycle of Anger Addiction

Anger can become addictive and can, therefore, cycle like any addiction. It is very similar to the cycle of addiction, except for one particular area. The parts of this cycle include: Strong Feelings, Telling Self Lies, Remembered Feelings and Believing Them, Use, Binge, Crisis, Emerge Remorseful, Solemn Resolves, Seeks Help, and finally Recovery.

As I said about the cycle of addiction, I believe this cycle is equally important to be recognized and addressed. There are some differences in this addiction, in that the second part of the cycle here is Remembered Feelings, as opposed to Remembered Pleasures, in the Cycle of Addiction. An angry person is not feeling pleasure, if dealing with it honestly.

Before participating in this activity in class, I pass out the cards to the students with the above words on them, asking each student how they identify with that part of the cycle, being sure everyone has a clear understanding of that part of anger.

As in class, I express to my students the importance of learning the order of the cycle. After thinking through each part and identifying what happens in each step, I ask them to visually look at the cycle one more time. Then, in a classroom setting, I ask the students to come up, a small group at the time, and help each other place the cards with the appropriate words on them in the correct order around the circle. When everyone has had a turn, we discuss the importance of learning this cycle, enabling them to hopefully break it before getting too far into the cycle.

I would now ask you to please draw a circle on paper, then put answers away, and try to write the words in the correct order of the cycle. If it would be of help to you, I encourage access to the words, just not in the correct order. That will be much more fun and challenging! If something is out of place, try again until it is all correct. If I am doing this and can admit I have an anger addiction problem, this simple activity might ultimately transform my life!

As far as knowing where to break this cycle, it will be the same as the Addiction Cycle, the Strong Feelings. This is where I do not have the strength to do it alone.   I feel extremely blessed to be able to turn to my higher power to renew and refresh my mind, and give me new strength to carry on.

Tool Two Confident Persuasive Message
Backpack

In our Anger Management Program, the **Backpack** is used as a manipulative to represent all the emotions we store in our subconscious mind. There are happy and sad emotions there. Some examples are: joy, happiness, confusion, trauma, pain, guilt, shame, blame, mistrust, doubt, misery, distress, lies, pride, rejection, and anger. Sometimes these emotions are triggered and bring to mind happy thoughts or thoughts of anger.

In class, I put on a **Backpack** for a visual effect of what happens with emotions in our subconscious mind. I ask the class these questions: can I see what is in the backpack, can I reach around and pull the emotions out, or will they just stay there my whole life and make me feel I will forever carry this load around? I then ask the students to write down on paper the emotions in their own backpacks. Then I explain: if I try each day to work on a negative emotion in my subconscious mind, asking my higher power to help me, it can be removed and replaced with a positive emotion. This might takes months of work and concentration, but the end result will be worth it.

At this time, I would like for you to write down all emotions you are carrying around in your own subconscious mind. You might think about the degree of hurt you feel as you read each one, and the effect they really have on your life. Then I would ask for you to circle one of the emotions that is the greatest burden to you, reminding yourself daily to work mentally on getting this out of your Backpack. I know it will take time, but with the help of your higher power, I know it is possible. Life is a choice and I believe you will choose to live your best life.   It is a rare and precious gift!

Tool Two
Confident Persuasive Message
The Message

The purpose of the Confident Persuasive Message is to communicate to someone your feelings in a manner that does not point fingers. It is meant to send a message with a goal to change a harmful behavior. There is no pre-conceived solution. It must be expressed honestly, with compassion and love. Someone receiving this message might be your wife, husband, boyfriend, girlfriend, mother, father, friend, etc. There is a formula used to fill in blanks about feelings, behavior, and the effect on one's life. The formula is:

...I feel_____(Disclose your real feelings)

...When_____(Non-judgmentally state the behavior)

...Because_____(Clarify the real effect on your life)

When I am teaching this in class, the first thing I do is write the formula on the chalkboard. I then ask for class participation to write at least six examples of how feelings need to be communicated in a way that is not accusing, but from the heart with deep, caring feelings. I do emphasize in the formula, that when expressing the behavior, it is done without using the word *you*. For example, "When you never help me with the children ..." That expressed feeling will bring on defensive behavior from the other person. A better example would be... "When I do not get enough help with our children ..."

A good example of a Confident Persuasive Message without using you could be the following:

I feel "disrespected"

When "opportunities to speak are not given to me"

Because "I know I have something to say that would help the situation."

The next step is for each class member to choose a feeling and write the formula. Each person then has a turn to share it with the class, therefore learning how to do this before leaving the classroom. I, as the instructor or another classmate, always offer help when needed. This is a great way to learn a tool that has the potential to be life changing.

For those doing this activity online, it is now time to take paper and pencil, choose a feeling, and then use the formula to practice putting your feelings on paper. Remember, the more practice, the better the message to someone will be. I would encourage practicing this with a friend before actually expressing your message to the concerned person. It is nice to learn to write positive messages as well as negative ones. I recommend writing at least four of each. If you have a family member or friend who would be willing to practice with you, this will enable you to learn this tool much faster. I think after a while, you will see the light as it relates to berating someone, as opposed to stating a message about your feelings and pain. I hope this is helpful in your journey.

Tool Three

Anger Log Optional Activities

I use the Anger Log as an instrument to write down

information that is relative to an anger event. This gives me an opportunity to become involved with expressing my anger on paper. As I record events, filling out at least three different anger events, I become aware of patterns. Perhaps I get angry when I am with certain people, at the same place, or anything else that is similar. I need to remember this tool to help me work with my anger. It is not a short term "fix it." Nevertheless, I consider it valuable, as I daily analyze my life and the progress I am making.

Tool Three

Anger Log

Recognizing Our Behavior

There are generally three kinds of behavior. The first I will discuss is **Submissive Behavior**. This behavior is **Most Yielding**. The second is **Assertive Behavior** which is **Most Decided**. The third is **Aggressive Behavior** which is **Most Demanding**. When I am teaching these behaviors and the characteristics of each behavior, I believe it is important to analyze myself as to the dominant behavior I usually express. I do have characteristics of all three, but I do have one that is dominant for me. As I recognize some of the behaviors I exhibit, but do not like about myself, then I have to work harder to get my behavior to a place I consider more acceptable.

I use an activity in class with my students to bring clarity to recognizing examples of certain behaviors. I pass out cards to the students with either the words **Submissive behavior**, **Assertive behavior**, or **Aggressive behavior** written on them. Then I read scenarios making reference to the different kinds of behavior. The students then hold up the card they think is correct for that scenario. I then ask the students the reason that behavior was chosen. I like to be sure there is understanding and not just guessing. An example of a scenario I might read would be...If you say that to me one more time, I'm going to hit you! Choosing Aggressive Behavior would be the correct answer because of the threatening words expressed. After I go through at least three examples of each behavior, the students are better prepared to recognize their own behavior and perhaps make some changes, if it is causing anger issues.

I am going to make up some scenarios related to the behaviors. I will be making reference to the characteristics of each behavior. Now it is your turn to take paper and pencil, choosing the answer you believe is correct for each one. You may refer to the characteristics of the behaviors, if need be. It will be more fun to try on your own and then check your answers on the next page.

1. If you don't do what I tell you to do, you had better watch your back!

2. I want to help you, but I don't want to invade in your space without your permission.

3. Just remember, when we are together as friends, I am in control!

4. I would love to have some new clothes, but I guess I should not spend money on myself.

5. I am so happy that my husband and I have a good relationship.

6. I will argue with you for hours about this, but I will have the final word!

7. I do not really want to help with the fundraiser, but I cannot tell anyone no.

8. My life is so fulfilled because I love helping others know the peace of my higher power.

9. Sometimes I would like to share what I think, but I just sit back and keep quiet.

Answers to the Behavior Scenarios:

1. Aggressive
2. Submissive
3. Aggressive
4. Submissive
5. Assertive
6. Aggressive
7. Submissive
8. Assertive
9. Submissive

Congratulations on the ones you answered correctly! You might want to look back over the characteristics of the behaviors to understand any incorrect answers that you may have given.

I hope this information is beneficial to you. As I went through the course for the first time, I understood my own behaviors much better. I have actually worked on changing some of them. It just takes personal thinking about the behaviors and exchanging them for a more assertive one. This will not happen overnight, but in time, it is possible!

Tool Three

Anger Log

Mismanagement Strategies

When I am teaching these mismanagement strategies in class, I initially discuss the meaning of each one.

The one I call the **Concealer** suppresses anger, bottles it up physically and does not deal with it.

The **Absorber** regularly talks negatively to self and in so doing, beats up on oneself.

The **Pretender** gets angry without being seen, wants to score and be funny.

The **Exploder** gets out of control quickly, his actions scare others, and these actions occur 80% of the time when fatigued or alcohol has been consumed.

After I sense there is a good understanding of all these wrong ways to handle anger, I use a manipulative to play a game, furthering their understanding of the strategies. Sometimes I put the students in groups to work together, and other times I let them work alone. I pass out cards with words referring to one of the strategies. I then read scenarios and the class members will respond by holding up the correct card. We then discuss the reason for their answer. By the time we are finished, I believe each student will definitely remember these strategies and recognize them in the future, knowing they are incorrect ways to handle anger.

Scenarios:

1. I wish I felt good about myself, but I do not think I am worthy of a good life.

2. You do that to me again, and I will hurt you!

3. I have been having so many headaches. I went to the doctor and found I also have high blood pressure. He said there is too much stress in my life.

4. How do you put up with that loser of a husband?

5. I wish I could talk about my anger, but I just keep it inside.

6. I wish I were as pretty as my best friend.

7. When I said you were looking older, I did not really mean it.

8. I do not ever want you leaving the house without my permission. You can never get away from me!

Now I would like you to read the scenarios and write down an answer beside the number. Refer to the definitions of each strategy before choosing an answer. After you are finished, you can check your answers below:

Answers to the Mismanagement Strategies:
1. Absorber
2. Exploder
3. Concealer
4. Pretender
5. Concealer
6. Absorber
7. Pretender
8. Exploder

I certainly saw myself more clearly after studying these strategies. I hope it is helpful to you in learning how not to handle your anger. Good luck to you as you progress through this class. Remember every day is new and we start each day with a clean slate.

Tool Three

Anger Log

Perverted Methods for Dealing with Anger

As I think about Perverted Methods and anger, I automatically know that these ways of dealing with anger are all incorrect. As I present these in class, I go over each one thoroughly so there is a good understanding of dealing with anger incorrectly!

The definition of each Perverted Method is as follows:

1. **Downsize it:** This kind of anger is automatic and instantaneous. This person will work very hard at not being angry.

2. **Postpone It:** This person delays feeling angry and responding to it. In addition, problems, conflicts, and decisions are delayed.

3. **Transfer It:** This is the process of removing anger from the person, place, or thing and putting it on a safer or less threatening person.

4. **Weaken It**: The anger is felt, but is diluted in an attempt to render the anger impotent.

5. **Exclude It**: One cannot feel with a frozen finger, and one cannot feel with frozen emotions.

After I thoroughly explain all these incorrect ways of handling anger, I use a manipulative in class for student participation. This encourages better understanding of how to let go of these incorrect ways of dealing with anger. I then pass out cards to everyone with the different Perverted Methods written on them. As I read a scenario, participants hold up the answer. We do discuss why it is correct or incorrect. Thus, I believe this provides a better understanding of all these incorrect ways to handle anger.

After reading these scenarios related to all of the Perverted Methods for Dealing with Anger, I would like for you to get a pencil and paper to write down what you believe is the correct answer for each scenario. After you finish, please look on the next page for the correct answers.

1. My husband just slapped me, but I am so grateful he is not walking out on me.

2. Judy, my best friend, just told me she does not want to go on the trip with me, and I have paid for both of us. I know I cannot be angry with her, but it makes me sad.

3. I found out my friend told a lie about me, but I will never confront her because she might not want to be my friend anymore.

4. I have told you not to spend so much time with people when helping them get their personal identification (ID). You could be helping other people. You are so hard-headed.

5. I am so angry at my husband for taking the children to a dangerous place. Maybe next weekend we can discuss it. That is just five days from now.

Learning all these perverted methods of dealing with anger have certainly awakened what I have done in the past. I will now be very aware of not doing them in the future. I am so thankful for this help with my life, and I hope it helps you too.

Answers to Five Perverted Methods for Dealing with Anger:
1. Weaken It
2. Downsize It
3. Exclude It
4. Transfer It
5. Postpone It

Tool Four

Responsible Model Optional Activities

Responsible Model

According to the dictionary, the word *responsible* means . . . accountable, as for something within one's power, having a capacity for moral decisions, capable of rational thoughts or actions, and showing reliability. As I teach this in class, I ask the students to ponder these thoughts: Self anger and guilt are mainly caused by our lack of responsibility. How can I be more responsible to myself with the help of my higher power? Not meeting my responsibilities makes those around me suffer. To be responsible, one must draw boundaries in her/his life. The lines define what you are and what you are not. This keeps the good in and the bad out. The bad stirs anger!

At this time in class, I introduce the people or things for which everyone is responsible. I purposefully list five people or things, leaving out two, and the class tries to decide which two are missing. After we become aware of everything that we are responsible for, I put laminated word cards on the wall in random order. I ask each student to have a turn placing the cards in the order of the way they see responsibility. Most of the time, everyone places the cards in a different order with a few similarities. As this continues, there is discussion about the reason for the order of placement. Dialogue is valuable to the understanding of being responsible.

In Random Order, The People and Things We are Responsible for are as follow:

Family
Friends
Extended Family
Country
Work
Higher Power
Animals
Myself

Now, I would ask you to write down the people or things in the order of responsibility in your life as you see it today. After you see the answers on the next page, perhaps you will have to change something. If so, I know your life will be better for it!

Correct Order is:

1. Higher power
2. Myself
3. The one closest to me (Spouse)
4. The one (s) next closest to me
5. The one (s) next closest to me
6. Etc.
7. Etc.

The other five can be in the order you want, reminding yourself, you do have responsibility for all in the list. We have found that as people learn more about responsibility, the vast majority will put their higher power first. The reason is that their present responsibility model is unacceptable and they must turn to a power greater than themselves.

Tool Six

High Way Journey Optional Activities

This is a powerful tool to use in life every day. It reminds me that I can be on different roads or paths in life. I know for myself, my journey in life has allowed me to experience being on all of them. The one I enjoy most is the **High Way.**

When I teach this tool in class, I go through the **Low Road**, explain the **Cycle of Belief**, the **Cycle Back Road, Mid-Way**, and the **High Way.** After thoroughly going over the characteristics of each road, I tell the students about a time in my life when I was on the High Way and moved very quickly to the Low Road. It is amazing how quickly things happen and how our belief system has a huge effect on where we find ourselves in life. This is my story.

After I had a heart attack in 2005, I was blessed with an amazing cardiologist. After a couple of years being under her care, she told me she was moving. She did recommend two other cardiologists. I chose one and made an appointment shortly after that, just to get to know him. On the assigned day, I went to see him. The first few minutes with him were spent giving me information about his life and his hobbies. Finally, he looked at my records and said he would like to add one low-dose prescription for high blood pressure. At the time, I was thinking to myself, I have low blood pressure. I usually ask questions, but that day I just had a feeling I would not be going back to him so I did not say anything. He then told me to go by the desk and make a follow-up appointment. When I approached the appointment desk, the lady asked me if the doctor commented about my giraffe necklace. I said no, but asked, why the question? She replied that the doctor goes on a hunting safari each year, has the head stuffed, and then brings them here to hang on the walls. The office I was in was the only one that didn't have a head hanging in it. I could feel my blood pressure rising and my muscles tightening up as I processed what this doctor had done to innocent animals in Africa. I was livid! The receptionist asked me again when I wanted to return for the next visit and I said, "I don't." I walked out.

Upon reflection, I completely ignored Tool One, **S-T-O-P** word, and Tool Two, Competent Persuasive Message Had I used these tools properly, I could have managed this negative anger correctly. At that time, using the lessons learned in this book, I made the decision to move on in a positive way with my higher power.

OPTIONAL
TOOL ONE TEST ANSWERS

1. Correct answer: C
2. Correct answer: B
3. Correct answer: A
4. Correct answer: D
5. Correct answer: D
6. Correct answer: B
7. Correct answer: C
8. Correct answer: B
9. Correct answer: D
10. Correct answer: A

TOOL TWO TEST ANSWERS

1. Correct answer: C
2. Correct answer: C
3. Correct answer: A
4. Correct answer: B
5. Correct answer: D
6. Correct answer: A
7. Correct answer: B
8. Correct answer: D
9. Correct answer: C
10. Correct answer: B

TOOL THREE TEST ANSWERS

1. Correct answer: C
2. Correct answer: C
3. Correct answer: C
4. Correct answer: D

5. Correct answer: A
6. Correct answer: B
7. Correct answer: A
8. Correct answer: A
9. Correct answer: C
10. Correct answer: B

TOOL FOUR TEST ANSWERS

1. Correct answer: A
2. Correct answer: A
3. Correct answer: B
4. Correct answer: A
5. Correct answer: C
6. Correct answer: B
7. Correct answer: C
8. Correct answer: D
9. Correct answer: C
10. Correct answer: A

TOOL FIVE TEST ANSWERS

1. Correct answer: C
2. Correct answer: C
3. Correct answer: B
4. Correct answer: A
5. Correct answer: A
6. Correct answer: D
7. Correct answer: C
8. Correct answer: A
9. Correct answer: B
10. Correct answer: C

TOOL SIX TEST ANSWERS

1. Correct answer: D
2. Correct answer: A
3. Correct answer: D
4. Correct answer: B
5. Correct answer: D
6. Correct answer: C
7. Correct answer: B
8. Correct answer: D
9. Correct answer: A
10. Correct answer: C

BIOGRAPHIES
JAY BURCHFIELD

Colonel (Retired) Joseph P. Burchfield, III retired from the United States Air Force after thirty years of honorable service with numerous honors. He served as a commander of two large intelligence units; Inspector General and Assistant Director of Operations for a world-wide Command; flew 100+ combat missions in the SEA conflict and hundreds of hours in the EB-47 and B-58 aircraft. He holds a Master of Arts in Lay Ministry from Southwestern Baptist Theological Seminary, Ft. Worth, TX; a Master of Arts in Management from Central Michigan University, Mt. Pleasant, MI; A Bachelor of Science from West Alabama University, Livingston, AL. From January 2001 to January 2004, he was the regional director of ASN. Since January 2004 he has been the executive director of Anger Solutions Network, Inc. (ASN). Currently he is an active deacon and Sunday school teacher at Trinity Baptist Church, a core member of the FCA Officials Huddle and a high school football official. He is married with two grown children and four grandchildren. Finally, he is a master, certified anger management, stress management and conflict resolution instructor/facilitator with ASN.

FRANK C. BOHANNAN

Frank "Bo" Bohannan spent his entire business career in the financial industry as a stockbroker and brokerage office manager with Dean Witter Reynolds (now Morgan Stanley). He graduated from Texas Western College (Now UTEP) in El Paso, Texas with a Bachelor of Business Administration. After retiring he became part of Anger Solutions Network and has facilitated various classes. He has held classes everywhere from the Bexar County Jail to classes in the Adult Education program of two school districts. He also spent five years as Director of Senior Adult Ministries at his church. He is one of the lead facilitators in developing and marketing Anger Solution Network's online learning program.

RAYMOND V. VELA

Raymond served in the military (U. S. Navy) Active and Reserves for twenty-five years. He was a Data Processor and intelligence specialist for the Fleet Intelligence Rapid Support Team out of Pearl Harbor. He attended Texas A & M with studies in business. He is an active church member in the Presbyterian Church (USA), has served as a Deacon and Elder in the Presbytery, Synod and the General Assembly. He worked in Civil Service and was a branch Chief in the Data Automation Division. He is currently a member of the Board of Directors for Anger Solutions Network and serves as the Treasurer and Special Projects Director. He is a facilitator teaching English and Spanish in a classroom environment.

GEORGE A. WALTON, JR

CMSGT (Retired) from the United States Air Force after thirty plus years of service. He served as an air policeman, equal opportunity investigator, human relations facilitator, and a substance abuse counselor. Mr. Walton also worked for the Texas Attorney General in the Child Support Division as a trainer, Director of Management Development, Director of Human Resources Development, litigation troubleshooter, Child Support Officer, and as a unit supervisor. The Bexar County Sheriff's Office used George's talents as a recruiter, human resources analyst, and commissioner. George now serves as: lead trainer for the Bexar County Dispute Resolution Center, member of the Bexar Senior Advisory Committee (performed as chairman in previous years) to the Alamo Area Council of Governments on senior citizens affairs, core member of the Celebrate Recovery (New Creation Christian Fellowship Church), member of Alamo Service Connection, Vice-Chair Shelf foundation, board member of Anger Solutions, and Sunday School teacher and deacon at RC Freedom Fellowship Christian Church. In addition, he is a skilled facilitator in training and mediation. He and his wife, Jessica, have six sons and fifteen grandchildren.

CYNTHIA FREEMAN

Cynthia taught elementary school for twenty-five years before retiring. She has always been involved in missions. In 2001, she and her husband volunteered to work at Ground Zero for two weeks under the

Ministry of Texas Baptist Men Disaster Relief. In 2008, Cynthia felt called to teach Anger Management to the ladies at Bexar County Jail. (She has also co-taught this class at The Brooklyn Tabernacle Learning Center, Brooklyn, NY.) In addition, she loves spending time with family, her two dachshunds (Brandy & Chocolate), friends, painting and taking photograph classes, which keeps her very busy and fulfilled.

LEATHA DAILEY GLISSON

Leatha Dailey Glisson is a graduate of the University of Oklahoma with a Master of Liberal Studies degree. A retired federal employee, she now writes creative nonfiction and is the author of two published books, *Some Glad Morning,* Parthena Press, 2001 and *Love Wears Many Faces,* Parthena Press, 2008. She is an active member of Trinity Baptist Church, San Antonio, Texas and writes the Living Legend column for the church's newsletter, The Trinity Trumpet. She enjoys mystery books and the many cultural activities in San Antonio.

REVEREND JAMES R. RYAN

James R. Ryan is a retired educator and United Methodist minister. His experience as an educator began at Starr Commonwealth for Boys, a home for orphaned and delinquent children in Michigan. Several levels of administration included elementary, middle school, and senior high school principal, and school superintendent. He taught at Trinity University in the Department of Education and served as an adjunct professor at Northwest Vista College. He graduated from Michigan State University with the degrees of B.A., M.A., and Ph.D. He has two daughters who hold positions in education and law, and five grandchildren, two who reside in San Antonio and three in Milwaukee.

BEN FREEMAN

Ben was a teacher, coach, education consultant, and administrator for 38 years in the public school system. In addition, he was a teaching associate at the University of Texas at San Antonio and Our Lady of the Lake University in San Antonio. Currently, he serves as a volunteer as the training director for the Texas Baptist Men Disaster Relief Program, an Anger Management and Conflict Resolution Trainer at the Haven for

Hope Homeless Shelter, and a design coordinator for the Trinity Baptist Church Mission Program. He spends time with his precious wife, children and grandchildren, two dachshunds – Brandy and Chocolate, attending sports activities, fishing and hunting with friends, and traveling. His greatest love is sharing his Christian faith with everyone – "It's All About Jesus"!!!!!

TROY LEBLANC

Troy is a veteran of Desert Storm and Desert Shield. After his military service, Troy served as an missionary from 1995-2007. Upon returning to the U.S., he founded and is the director of Elyon Media Group LLC, a local Christian media production company that serves corporate, charities, ministries and missions with media. He is also the founder of the San Antonio Kid's Film Festival and Elyon Media Academy, a film and media program mentoring youth in discipleship in Christ and entrepreneurship. Troy is a music recording artists and is, through his studio, providing internships and a platform for undiscovered artist to have a venue to share their music, art and visual media with the world.

RENEE SMITH

Renee graduated with a Bachelor's degree from Stanford University in Palo Alto, California and received her Juris Doctor and Master of Business Administration degrees from the University of California Los Angeles. Renee joined Mellon Bank in 1984 as a corporate lender and held various other banking positions. She retired as a Global Risk Management and Compliance Manager at the Bank of New York Mellon Corporation. While engaged in her banking careers in Pennsylvania and Massachusetts, Renee volunteered her free time working with various charitable organizations. Most of her activities involved teaching leadership skills to teenagers and mentoring troubled young adults. Currently, Renee is an adjunct instructor at St. Philip's College in San Antonio, Texas. She volunteers her time as a facilitator with Anger Solutions Network, a greeter at the McNay Art Museum in San Antonio, and studies Bible doctrine. She is a member of Trinity Baptist Church in San Antonio.

SANDEE MEWHINNEY JOHNS

Born in San Antonio, Sandee is a proud 5th generation Texan. She graduated from Alamo Heights High School, Texas State University and Our Lady of the Lake University. She taught 11th grade English and was librarian at Robert G. Cole High School. Two of her former students were Alan Keyes and Shaquille O'Neal. She ended her 40-year teaching/librarian duties with 13 years at Holmes High School. She is an avid reader and belongs to three book clubs. She has a Dewey classified library of 2000 books in her upstairs den. Travel has always been her passion. She began traveling when she graduated from college and has been going since then. She has been to the seven continents and to 109 countries. She was fortunate to have lived a year, each, in Ottawa, Canada and Melbourne, Australia, on teaching exchanges. She is married to David, who has traveled to 92 countries with her. She enjoys his seven grandchildren. They are rescue owners of Lily, a 12-year-old dachshund. Sandee is a big Fiesta fan. For the past four years, she has had a medal made in honor of her son, Preston, who was 25 when killed by a drunk driver. Sandee is a big collector of Fiesta medals, collecting 408 this past year. She has been a member of Trinity Baptist Church for 62 years and enjoys volunteering on various committees. She is co-director of "That Class" Sunday School class, where she was fortunate to get to know Jay Burchfield.

From Anger To Contentment

Published by
Elyon Media Group LLC
Studio: 210.473.5182
www.elyonmedia.com
ISBN-13:
978-0692718339
(Elyon Media Group LLC)
ISBN-10:
0692718338

Made in the USA
San Bernardino, CA
01 June 2016